ARMISTICE
1918

The History of the Cameronians (Scottish Rifles), 1933–1946.
The London Scottish in the Second World War—1939 to 1945.
History of The Royal Northumberland Fusiliers in the Second World War.
The History of The Duke of Wellington's Regiment, 1919 to 1952.
The Regimental History of the 3rd Queen Alexandra's Own Gurkha Rifles, 1927–1947.
The History of The Sherwood Foresters, 1919–1957.
History of the 16th/5th The Queens Royal Lancers, 1925–1961.
The First Commonwealth Division (Korea, 1950–3).
The History of the 53rd (Welsh) Division in the Second World War.
The New Warfare.
Against Great Odds (the story of the first offensive in Libya in 1940–1).
On Their Shoulders: British Generalship in the Lean Years, 1939–1942.
Battle 1066.
Part-time Farmer.
Editor, *The Army Quarterly and Defence Journal*, 1950–1966.
Army Editor, *Brasseys Annual, The Armed Forces Year Book* (since 1950).

ARMISTICE
1918

Brigadier C. N. Barclay
C.B.E., D.S.O.

SOUTH BRUNSWICK
NEW YORK: A. S. BARNES AND COMPANY

ARMISTICE 1918. © Text, Brigadier C. N. Barclay, 1968, © Maps, J. M. Dent & Sons Ltd, 1968. First American edition published 1969 by A. S. Barnes and Company, Inc., Cranbury, New Jersey 08512

Library of Congress Catalogue Card Number:
72-81683

SBN 498 07376 9

Printed in the United States of America

ACKNOWLEDGEMENTS

My thanks are due to so many people who advised and helped me in compiling this book that I could not possibly name them all. Prominent among them are Mr W. D. King, O.B.E., the Librarian, Central Library, Ministry of Defence, and his staff; Brigadier J. Stephenson, O.B.E., the Director and the Library Staff, Royal United Service Institution; and Dr Noble Frankland, D.F.C., M.A., D.PHIL., the Director, and the Photographic Library Staff, of the Imperial War Museum, all of whom gave me valuable assistance in selecting photographs.

I am also indebted to the publishers, Messrs J. M. Dent & Sons Ltd, for their courtesy and help, especially to Mr Michael Geare, who first put the idea of writing a book of this kind into my head, and subsequently gave me a number of useful tips.

I also owe a lot to Miss P. C. McGlinchy of Camberley, who has typed this and other scripts for me over a period of thirty-five years and never once failed to deliver the goods by the appointed day!

Probably the most valuable impressions and items of information came from a number of friends of my own generation who were serving on the Western Front in 1918, and to whom I express my special thanks. One of them—recently deceased—served in France with an infantry battalion throughout the war—from September 1914 until November 1918.

v

Acknowledgements are also made to the authors, editors and publishers of the following, from which a few short quotations have been made in some cases, and background information obtained:

History of the Great War. Military Operations France and Belgium 1918, volumes IV and V (the Official Histories), compiled by Brigadier-General Sir James E. Edmonds, C.B., C.M.G., HON. D.LITT. (Oxon). (HMSO.)

A Short History of World War I by Brigadier-General Sir James E. Edmonds, C.B., C.M.G., HON. D.LITT. (Oxon). (Oxford University Press, 1951.)

The Annual Register for 1919. (Longmans, Green, 1920.)

A History of the Peace Conference of Paris, volume I. Edited by H. W. V. Temperley. (Henry Frowde and Hodder & Stoughton, 1920.)

Douglas Haig as I Knew Him, by G. S. Duncan, O.B.E., D.D., LL.D. (George Allen and Unwin, 1966.)

The Kaiser and his Court: the Diaries, Note Books and Letters of Admiral Georg Alexander von Müller, Chief of the Naval Cabinet, 1914–1918, edited by Walter Görlitz. (Macdonald, English translation, 1961.)

1918. The Last Act, by Barrie Pitt. (Cassell, 1962.)

The World Crisis 1911–1918, by the Rt Hon. Winston S. Churchill, O.M., C.H., M.P. (Odhams Press, 1938 edition.)

My War Memories 1914–1918, by General Ludendorff. (Hutchinson, English translation, 1919.)

The Army Quarterly and Defence Journal. (William Clowes.)

Britain Between the Wars, 1918–1940, by Charles Loch Mowat. (Methuen, 1955.)

C. N. B.

CONTENTS

ILLUSTRATIONS

All photographs are reproduced by permission of the Imperial War Museum

War is much too serious a thing to be left to military men!

(Briand, quoting Talleyrand to Lloyd George during the First World War.)

It may be that some Frenchmen said that war was too serious a matter to be left to generals. What is even more obvious is that peace is much too difficult for politicians to handle.

(Extract from a letter received by the author in 1965.)

AUTHOR'S PREFACE

Many thousands of books have been written about the First World War of 1914–18, and to many it must seem that there is little to add. It was, however, suggested to me that the circumstances of the Armistice which ended the fighting had escaped close attention; and on investigating the more important and obvious literature on the subject I came to the same conclusion. I therefore decided to write a book, for the general reader, explaining how the cease-fire came about, its immediate repercussions and its long-term influence on the world today. The idea had a special appeal for me because I still possess some notes, which I had made soon after the Armistice, giving my impressions of events—very clumsily written but invaluable in refreshing my memory. Publication in the half-century anniversary year seemed very appropriate.

A notable feature of the Armistice of 11th November 1918, and one which crops up frequently in this book, was its unexpectedness. In June and July, and even in August of that year, most well-informed people in Allied countries believed that a continuation of the war well into 1919 was almost certain. The reasons for, and events which brought about, the early termination of hostilities make an interesting study. They not only involve military operations and political moves on a grand scale, but also introduce some of the most colourful personalities of the twentieth century—Lloyd George, Clemenceau, Haig, Foch, Pétain, Kaiser William II, Hindenburg, Ludendorff, Woodrow Wilson, Winston Churchill and others.

My knowledge of basic events has been gleaned from official records and from published works: but much of the detail is from my own recollection of events and from the recollections of many friends of my own generation whose brains I have picked. The short character sketches of Allied leading figures, with the exception of Pétain and Woodrow Wilson, represent the views and impressions of people who actually knew them and were given to me personally.

I have not cluttered the text with a lot of source references or footnotes, but I can give an assurance that all facts have been carefully verified: where doubt exists it has been stated. I, of course, accept full responsibility for the opinions expressed on controversial matters. I have not written primarily for scholars or military historians who are specialists of the period. My aim has been to tell ordinary educated people, in simple English, the main facts concerning events which have had, and will continue to have, an incalculable influence on the lives of all of us.

In recent years a lot has been written in adverse criticism of the generals of the First World War; not by people who actually participated—who might be expected to be most critical—but by a younger generation of men whose information comes to them second-hand. I do not doubt the sincerity of most of these writers, some of whom are distinguished historians: but I think that many have failed to make proper allowance for the conditions in which the commanders of 1914–18 operated; and maybe that to expect them to do so is asking too much. Unlike their successors of 1939–45 the generals of 1914–18 had not been young officers in a previous national war and had not at their disposal the accumulated experience of that war; they did not have the open flanks and fluid operations of World War II to display their skill; they did not possess the tanks and aircraft which gave the offensive the advantage over the defensive and they were not supported by a man of Winston Churchill's calibre in the early years of fighting.

Judged by man's life-span fifty years is a long time. A historian, writing in 1964 or 1965 about events in 1914–18, is almost exactly comparable as regards time-lag with one writing during the American Civil War (1861–65) about the Battle of Waterloo (1815). In the American War they had the telegraph and railways: at Waterloo the railway was undreamt of and there was no cable or telegraph. (Indeed, it is said that the first news of the Waterloo victory arrived in London by carrier pigeon.) Yet the inventions and developments between 1914 and 1964 were vastly greater than between 1815 and 1865. Many military writers of the present decade or so, writing about World War I, have given insufficient attention to the difference in circumstances due to a lapse of nearly half a century.

Criticism has been levelled at the generals of all the major powers involved in World War I. In particular Lord Haig has been selected as a target for abuse. It is not the main purpose of this book to rescue reputations which have come under fire; but I have found it necessary, as part of the Armistice story, to defend Haig. No student of military history would put Haig among the select company of Great Captains. He had some shortcomings, but he also possessed many of the finest qualities of the British race and, as I hope I have been able to show, it was he, more than any other man, who pointed the way to victory in 1918, instead of letting the war drag on into 1919.

There are three points in connection with the construction of this book which I would like to make clear.

Firstly—I may, quite justifiably, be accused of some repetition. In most cases this is deliberate, in order to emphasize something which I regard as being of special importance. The unexpectedness of the Armistice, Foch's strategic design, Haig's grasp of the tactical situation and the conspicuous part played by Rawlinson's Fourth Army in the final advance—these are a few examples of this conscious repetition.

Secondly—although this is a book dealing with the Western Front as a whole, and the events surrounding the Armistice of November 1918, some slight emphasis falls on the British. This is not entirely because I am British and writing mainly for

English-speaking people, but also because in the final stages of
the fighting British forces played the major part.

Lastly—I should like to explain the circumstances in which I
came to take a special interest in the events of the Armistice
period. In 1918 I was serving in Mesopotamia (now Iraq) and
was wounded near Mosul on the day of the Armistice with
Turkey (30th October 1918). Subsequently I spent some three
months in hospital in Baghdad, Basra and Bombay, and in a
convalescent hostel for officers at Nasik (near Bombay).
During this time the Armistice with Germany, and the first
moves in the return to peace, came about. The English language
Indian papers and the English papers we received were full of
news on these matters. I spent a good deal of my time reading,
making notes and discussing with others the last battles of the
war and the current topics of the day. A good deal of what I
have written in this book originates from these notes.

                                                C. N. BARCLAY.

London,
January 1968.

CHRONOLOGY

Important Dates of the Armistice Period, 1918–1919

1918

26 MARCH   Conference of Allied leaders held at Doullens to
              consider measures necessary in view of the
              alarming success of the German offensive in the
              Amiens area, which had begun on 21 March.
              General Ferdinand Foch appointed Supreme Com-
              mander of the Allied Armies.

15 JULY   Beginning of the Second Battle of the Marne
              (15 July to 6 August), when the Germans made
              the last of their series of spring and summer
              offensives.

18 JULY   German attack halted and, in face of French
              counter-offensive, they began withdrawing
              from the bridge-head gained south of the River
              Marne.

6 AUGUST   The French counter-offensive, which had driven
              the Germans back to the north bank of the River
              Vesle, came to a halt. *This ended the Second Battle*
              of the Marne—the turn of the tide, in that the German
              attacks ceased and the Allies went over to the offensive.

8–11 AUGUST   The Battle of Amiens. The French First Army on the right and General Rawlinson's British Fourth Army on the left advanced on a front of fifty miles. A great success. German casualties over 75,000. *This operation opened Ludendorff's eyes to the sharp decline in German morale and fighting spirit, and convinced Haig that victory was attainable in 1918.*

20 AUGUST
TO
10 SEPTEMBER   Series of Allied attacks took place, with uniform success, known by a variety of names—Battles of Bapaume, Arras, Albert, Scarpe and Drocourt–Quéant Line.

12–14
SEPTEMBER   First major operation by American troops—the successful attack on, and reduction of, the Saint Mihiel Salient.

12–26
SEPTEMBER   British Third and Fourth Armies attack and gain footing in Hindenburg Position.

27 SEPTEMBER   The series of Allied offensive operations which were to end the war—the Advance to Victory—began.

29 SEPTEMBER   Bulgaria granted an Armistice by the Allies.

OCTOBER   The Allied Armies advanced steadily eastwards.

1 OCTOBER   Prince Max of Baden became the German Imperial Chancellor. Hindenburg demanded that an immediate request for an Armistice be made.

4 OCTOBER   Note sent by Germany to the American President, Woodrow Wilson, asking terms on which Allies would grant an Armistice.

8 OCTOBER   President Wilson, in a speech, announced his celebrated 14 points (*see* Appendix A) as a basis for ending the war and securing a lasting peace.

27 OCTOBER   Resignation of General Ludendorff, who was succeeded by General Gröner.

29 OCTOBER   Mutinies and ill-discipline in the German Navy, which had been brewing for some time, became manifest.

30 OCTOBER   Turkey granted an Armistice by the Allies. Workers throughout Germany, who had been showing signs of unrest for some time, intensified their demands for peace. Prince Max and Hindenburg came to the conclusion that there was a danger of open revolution.

NOVEMBER   During the remaining days of war (1 to 11 November) the Allies continued to press forward on the Western Front against decreasing, yet still formidable, opposition.

4 NOVEMBER   Austria granted an Armistice by the Allies.

6 NOVEMBER   General Gröner (Ludendorff's successor) informed the Chancellor that the military situation was desperate, and that an Armistice must be negotiated by 9 November at the latest. In the evening the Allied governments informed Berlin by wireless that Marshal Foch had been authorized to receive representatives of the German government and inform them of the terms on which an Armistice would be granted.

NIGHT 7–8   The German Armistice Delegation crossed the
NOVEMBER   front line.

8 NOVEMBER   Thirty senior front line German officers, assembled in Spa, stated unanimously that the German Army could not be relied upon to suppress a revolution.

9 NOVEMBER   At 2 p.m. a republic was proclaimed for the whole of Germany and Herr Ebert took over the Chancellorship from Prince Max.

10 NOVEMBER   During the early hours Kaiser William II, on
              Hindenburg's advice, left Spa for Holland,
              crossing the frontier at Eysden at about 8 a.m.

11 NOVEMBER   *The Armistice agreement was signed at 5.5 a.m.
              and at 11 a.m. all fighting ceased (see Appendix B).*

28 NOVEMBER   The Kaiser signed an act of abdication,
              renouncing the Crowns of Prussia and Imperial
              Germany.

1919

28 JUNE   The Peace Treaty between the Associated
              Powers and Germany (the Treaty of Versailles,
              1919) was signed at Versailles (*see* Appendix C).

1

BACKGROUND

(SEE MAPS I, V)

Great events cannot be considered properly in isolation. It is essential to know in broad outline the circumstances in which they were framed. The Armistice of 1918 is no exception. It was the culmination of more than four years of total world war, and was brought about by a series of highly complicated military and political events involving a number of colourful personalities.

It is the object of this opening chapter to provide the background to the main story.

THE NATURE OF AN ARMISTICE

A well-known English dictionary defines the word 'Armistice' as 'A suspension of hostilities', and that is exactly what it is. The word was not in general use, indeed it was unfamiliar to many people, before the autumn of 1918. On the previous occasion when Britain and one of her enemies had stopped fighting—in South Africa in May 1902—the word 'peace' had been used as a general term for both the military cease-fire and the political settlement, and that was the word most people expected to hear when the German war came to an end.

To those with the task of considering these matters it became clear by about the middle of 1917 that the gigantic struggle which had begun in 1914 could not be resolved in a matter of weeks after the last shot had been fired, but only after much discussion and hard bargaining, not only with the ex-enemy, but also among Allies and perhaps with neutrals. This agreement—the Peace Treaty—would be chiefly a matter for politicians; the arrangements for a cease-fire, and the intervening period before the signing of the Peace Treaty, would be mainly a military affair, to be known as the Armistice.

And so, in the autumn of 1918, this previously little-known word came into use. Since then it has become familiar to many millions in all parts of the world, when once a year men and women assemble at places of worship, and memorials, to pay tribute to the fallen of two world wars. In Britain, and other parts of the Commonwealth, the Armistice Day services and parades have become an annual pilgrimage.

Theoretically an Armistice is reached by negotiation between the warring countries: in actual practice it is more often granted by the winning side on a plea from the side on the point of defeat. To 'sue for an Armistice' is the customary phrase. This request need not necessarily be direct to the opposing military commander. In 1918 the Germans made their request through Woodrow Wilson, the President of the United States, mainly because they thought him more likely to be sympathetic towards their case than the head of any other Allied country.

At the time of, or rather just before, the cessation of hostilities the German Army was still intact—a much weakened force, but still capable of offering stubborn resistance for a time. The German request for an Armistice was to prevent the inevitable collapse and eventual disintegration of her army; and permit the troops to march home in good order for the purpose of mitigating the outward signs of defeat and to help preserve law and order and the fabric of a stable society.

In these circumstances the main aim of the Allied Armistice terms was to impose conditions which would cripple the German Army as a fighting force and make it incapable of resuming the contest. We therefore find—as will be explained later in Chapter VII—that the main feature of the terms was the immediate surrender of a large quantity of war material—aircraft, guns, tanks, mortars, etc., and also warships, in sufficient quantities to virtually disarm the enemy.

SUMMARY OF THE MAJOR EVENTS IN 1918

The German armies on the Western Front, reinforced by some 44 divisions from the Russian Front, carried out a series of offensives, commencing on 21st March and ending in July. These operations, although they appeared at times to be on the point of success, failed in their object of attaining a decisive victory and gained only vulnerable salients and heavy casualties for the Germans. On 18th July the Allies began the great counter-offensive, and series of advances, which resulted in an Armistice on 11th November.

On the Eastern Front hostilities had ceased on 2nd December 1917 and the Peace Treaty of Brest-Litovsk was signed between Germany and the Bolsheviks on 3rd March 1918. In the early autumn Germany's allies began to collapse. On 29th September the Bulgarians applied direct for a cease-fire to the Allied commander in the Mediterranean; on the 30th October hostilities against Turkey came to an end and on 4th November the Austrian request for an Armistice from Italy was granted.

By the first days of November 1918 Germany found herself confronted by the three most powerful nations in the world, without allies and with her armies retreating rapidly eastwards towards the Fatherland. Germany had started negotiations for an Armistice as early as 4th October, but when the cease-fire actually came on 11th November it amounted, for all practical purposes, to unconditional surrender.

PERSONALITIES

Although wars have ceased to be dynastic they still revolve round personalities.

Napoleon dominated the wars of his age and it is perhaps true to say that no war has ever produced four such outstanding personalities as Churchill, Roosevelt, Stalin and Hitler. Also from World War I—particularly in its later stages—there emerged names which will live as long as history remains recorded—Lloyd George, Clemenceau, Foch, Haig, Woodrow Wilson, Hindenburg, Ludendorff and others. For a proper

study of the events to be described it is necessary to know
something about these men and the part they played in the
story of their times.

On the European continent, particularly in the countries of
the two chief rivals—France and Germany—the problems of
war, although immensely complicated in detail, were simple
in outline: in the case of France to fight Germany; in the case
of Germany to fight France in the West with the almost
certainty of also having to fight Russia on her Eastern frontier.
The armies to fight this war existed in peace and had only to
be mobilized to start hostilities. Those concerned had the
experience of the War of 1870–71 to guide them. In Britain it
was very different. She had no experience of modern war
between national forces supplied by railways; she had no army
available to fight on a continental scale; for her the war would
be a mainly naval one in its early stages.

By 1918 all this had changed. The war had not gone in the
manner predicted by the pundits: it had become a contest of
attrition which bedevilled the generals in their efforts to find a
solution to the deadlock. The early leaders of the warring
nations had mostly left the stage and been replaced by others.

By the early summer the Allied political scene was dominated
by three men—David Lloyd George, the British Prime
Minister; Georges Clemenceau, the seventy-seven-year-old
Premier of France; and Woodrow Wilson, the President of the
United States, whose influence was increasing rapidly as his
country's war effort expanded. On the military side Foch, who
had been appointed co-ordinating Generalissimo of the Allied
Armies in March 1918, was in public estimation the outstanding figure. In limited subordination to him were the two
Commanders-in-Chief, Haig and Pétain, whose battered
armies were recovering from the mauling they had received in
the German spring offensive. As the commander of the expanding American forces, General Pershing, like his President,
enjoyed an increasing voice in the conduct of affairs. If the war
was to continue until mid-1919, as most people believed, his
troops would decide the issue.

In Germany the Kaiser was still nominally the Head of State

and Supreme War Lord. In fact the country's policies and destinies had for some time been in the hands of the two soldiers—Field-Marshal von Hindenburg and General Erich Ludendorff. At the end of September, when all hope of a German victory had been abandoned, Prince Max of Baden was made Chancellor in the hope that his well-known Liberal views would make him acceptable to the Allies as a peace negotiator.

The Allied leadership included men of a wide range of experience and varied temperament. Lloyd George, the typical politician, exuded energy; a confirmed 'Easterner', he believed that the war was to be won elsewhere than on the Western Front, but he was never strong enough to carry his strategic views against Clemenceau, Foch, Robertson and Haig, who were all convinced that the Western Front was the decisive theatre. Haig, the British Commander-in-Chief on the Western Front, was a solitary figure. Rarely seeing eye to eye with his political masters and often at loggerheads with the French generals, he, nevertheless, managed to steer a course which enabled him to implement his conviction that he, and he alone, was destined to lead the British armies to final victory. To his troops he was a remote and knightly figure; handsome, always immaculately dressed, dignified—he embodied their conception of a British general and a Scottish laird. Among politicians, and probably to the dynamic and quick-witted Foch, he sometimes appeared obstinate to the point of stupidity. Yet, as we shall see as the story of the Armistice period unfolds, it was probably Haig, more than any other individual, who brought hostilities to an end in 1918 rather than in 1919.

To these leading British figures must be added two others. Winston Churchill as First Lord of the Admiralty had played a leading part in preparing the Fleet for war and in the affairs of the Royal Navy in the opening stages of hostilities. But in May 1915, as a result of major political changes, he had left the Admiralty. From November 1915 until the autumn of 1916 he was a front-line infantry officer on the Western Front, for most of the time commanding the 6th Battalion The Royal Scots Fusiliers. At the time of the events described in this book he was

Minister of Munitions. Another personality of note was General
Sir Henry Wilson, who had succeeded General Sir William
Robertson as Chief of the Imperial General Staff in February
1918. Previous to this he had been the British Representative at
the Supreme War Council. Earlier in the war he had rarely
seen eye to eye with Haig, and from the latter's War Diaries *
it would seem that the two men had a mutual antipathy
towards each other; but they seem to have co-operated reasonably well in 1918.

In France the leaders were a varied assortment. Clemenceau
(known as 'The Tiger'), in spite of his seventy-seven years, was
the main driving force, oozing energy and determination.
Eccentric in appearance and habits, and an agnostic, he had,
nevertheless, captivated the French people and their Allies by
his personality and will to win whatever the difficulties and
cost.

Unlike many French generals Marshal Foch had no colonial
experience. He had spent most of his military career in France,
and had made a deep study of modern continental warfare,
with particular reference to the problems which would face
France in the event of another war with Germany. He was a
devout Roman Catholic, and it is interesting to note that when,
in 1908, he was made Director of the *École de Guerre* the appointment was due mainly to the influence of Clemenceau—the anti-
cleric. The story is told that one day during the heat of battle in
1918 Clemenceau visited Foch's headquarters, to be told that
the Marshal was at prayers. 'Do not disturb him,' said the
Premier; 'if that sort of thing helps him in his duties I have no
wish to interfere with him.' †

Foch was by nature impetuous and perhaps too hasty in
making decisions; but, like his political master, he inspired
confidence and enthusiasm wherever he went. As Supreme
director of operations he was perhaps fortunate in having as his
subordinates two men like Haig and Pétain who, whilst working

* See *The Private Papers of Douglas Haig—1914–1919*, edited by Robert
Blake.

† This story has been repeated over the years. It has proved difficult to
verify, but seems to have a basis of truth.

loyally under his guidance, were not afraid to question his decisions and opinions, and were less prone to hasty judgement than their more volatile chief.

In Britain today Marshal Pétain is remembered mostly for his part in the French surrender in 1940. He deserves better than that: it is more fitting to remember him as the defender, and victor, of Verdun in 1916, and as the man who pulled the French Army together in 1917 after the widespread mutinies which followed the disastrous Nivelle offensive. These were achievements which may well have averted an Allied defeat in World War I: his part in the surrender of 1940 was not decisive: it would have happened whoever had been at the head of affairs in France at that time. In temperament he was a placid and dignified figure, outwardly cold towards his subordinates, but a highly trained and shrewd soldier. In 1918 he was probably as much like Haig in character as any Frenchman can be like a Scotsman.

The two leading Americans—Woodrow Wilson, the President, and General Pershing, the Commander of the American troops in France—were in a very special position. Wilson was an idealist with a faith in human nature that was not always realistic and a greater belief in his influence over his own countrymen than was justified. His country's late entry into the war (6th April 1917), vital as it was to the Allied cause, gave to him an aura of impartiality in what many others besides Americans regarded as a European contest. This enabled him to negotiate the Armistice, based on his famous 14 points,* in a manner which was not open to any other leading world figure. Without his part in the negotiations passions might have got out of hand, and the Armistice have been a less orderly affair than it was. It was a sad end to Wilson's public life to see his countrymen repudiate the League of Nations which he had done so much to found.

General Pershing found himself in a very curious position in

* Actually the 14 points were mostly concerned with the eventual Peace Terms, which was a political matter. They had little direct bearing on the Armistice, which was a military agreement. The 14 points are given in detail in Appendix A.

the first half of 1918. With no practical experience of modern
warfare, and belonging to an army which had not contemplated land warfare on the scale being waged in Europe, he was
at the head of a force which held the balance between victory
and defeat. His Franco-British Allies could only carry out their
offensive policy for victory in the knowledge that their inevitable casualties would be made good by reinforcements from
America. Moreover, if the war continued into 1919 Pershing's
force would number some 80 divisions, and be the Allies'
strongest national contingent. In these conditions he found
himself surrounded by British and French generals—one of
whom was his generalissimo—who had been at war for nearly
four years—although he might have been excused in thinking
that they had not been conspicuously successful in bringing the
contest to a satisfactory conclusion! His difficulties in Europe
were increased by political conditions in America where public
opinion was by no means unanimously in favour of intervention
in the war. His President, Congress and the American people
expected him to be sparing with American lives, and national
pride expected the American forces in Europe to fight as one
army, not with their divisions mixed up with British and French
divisions under foreign commanders. Few generals have had a
more delicate task than Pershing in 1918.

In appearance, character and manner the American
Commander-in-Chief belied the popular conception of an
American of those days. He was an athletic type of middle-aged
man of dignified appearance and invariably immaculately
turned out. He was firm in manner, but always polite, and
showed none of the flamboyance commonly associated with his
countrymen by Europeans. Haig wrote in his diary after their
first meeting, apparently with some surprise, 'I was much
struck with his quiet gentlemanly bearing—so unusual for an
American. Most anxious to learn, and fully realizes the great-
ness of the task before him.'

Lloyd George is supposed to have said on first meeting him,
'He might well be a British general'—not necessarily a compli-
ment from that quarter!

It is interesting to note that Haig describes Pershing's A.D.C.,

Captain George Patton, as a 'fire-eater, and longs for a fray'. He was to become better known as the commander of the American Third Army in 1944–45, which led the way across France in the assault on Hitler's Germany.

As was to be expected Pershing had differences of opinion with both Foch and Haig, mainly on the question of the command of American troops. But, on the whole, there were surprisingly few disagreements, and Pershing carried out his very difficult task with tact, understanding and not an inconsiderable degree of professional skill. Surprisingly it was in the administrative field that the American forces showed weakness. They fought with skill and courage, but Foch complained that units often went without supplies for several days, and consequently men were found wandering about all over the place looking for food.

In considering the Allied personalities we should not overlook the gallant King Albert of the Belgians, who remained to the end in personal command of the not inconsiderable Belgian Army, after all but a very small slice of his country had been overrun by the Germans.

Military leaders tend to run in pairs. In the Napoleonic Wars the Emperor and Berthier, styled 'Prince of staff officers' by his master; Roberts and Kitchener in the South African War; Mongtomery and de Guingand in World War II, are a few examples of many. In World War I it was Hindenburg and Ludendorff on the German side. This famous, but perhaps somewhat over-rated, pair came into prominence for their spectacular victory over the Russians in East Prussia in 1914. Towards the end of the war they attained considerable political influence as well as control of the armed forces. Gradually Hindenburg—in his seventy-second year in 1918—became a figurehead, a status which he continued to enjoy as President after the war. Ludendorff was the brains of the partnership; among the many devices to secure a German victory was his introduction of new tactical methods for the Western Front during the spring offensive of 1918. A dour and unattractive man, he attained limited successes, but was unable to provide the recipe for decisive victory. His last important act of the war was to advise the German Government to ask the Allies for an Armistice.

THE GERMAN OFFENSIVE IN THE
SPRING AND EARLY SUMMER OF 1918

The year 1917 was marked by two events which, more than any others, were to influence the course of the war in its final stages.

The first was the Russian Revolution which began on 12th March 1917 and brought about a cease-fire on the Eastern Front on 2nd December 1917, followed by a Peace Treaty in March 1918.

The second was the entry of the United States into the war on 6th April and the build-up of American forces in France, which began with the arrival of the first contingent on 25th June 1917.

It did not require an intimate knowledge of strategy, or even a very high standard of intelligence, to realize that these two events could prove crucial to the outcome of the war. The cease-fire on the Eastern Front would release some 44 German divisions for operation in the West and by the spring of 1918 give them a numerical advantage over the Allies which could bring them victory. But this advantage would be fleeting: if the war continued beyond the summer of 1918 the German armies would have to face ever-increasing numbers of American troops and quantities of equipment, and this in the end was bound to prove decisive.

There were other reasons why an early German bid for victory was indicated. The French armies were still suffering from the failure and losses of the Nivelle offensive and the widespread mutinies which followed. The British Army had not yet recovered from the abortive offensives which culminated at Passchendaele (October and November 1917) and Cambrai (November and December 1917), staged very largely to relieve pressure on the French whose front—mercifully unknown to the German High Command—was practically undefended for a period at the height of the mutinies. In these circumstances the Allies were not likely to be able to mount an offensive which would anticipate one by the Germans.

If anything can ever be regarded as certain in war it was the pattern of the coming campaign on the Western Front as seen in the closing days of 1917. A massive German spring offensive was to be expected; an all-out bid for victory before the Americans arrived in force. By the Allies every possible effort would be made to hold the enemy at bay against the day when overwhelming American, British and French armies would batter the exhausted enemy to pieces.

At the beginning of January 1918 the number of British and Dominion divisions on the Western Front was 57, a gain of one since January 1917; but the strength in fighting personnel had fallen from 1,192,668 to 1,097,906 during the same period. The drop in strength was mostly in the British infantry, which Haig estimated would be some 40 per cent below establishment by 31st March unless further drafts from home could be made available.

A worse situation existed in the French Army, which Pétain reported was losing about 40,000 men per month with little prospects of improvement. In the closing weeks of 1917 he had reduced the number of divisions from 109 to 100 and the infantry establishment per division from 7,200 to 6,000.

On the other hand the German strength had been gradually increasing throughout the latter months of 1917, as divisions were released from the Russian Front. By Christmas 1917 the number of divisions was 162, and it was to rise to 195 by 21st March 1918 when their great offensive began. The establishment of a German division in infantry was, however, only 5,850, but this was compensated by having a much greater number of trench mortars and machine-guns than Allied divisions.

In Haig's command various measures were introduced resulting from the shortage of infantry, the most drastic being the reduction of the number of infantry battalions in the division from twelve to nine. This meant reducing each brigade from four to three battalions, which in turn involved a change in tactics—best described as from a 'square' to a 'triangular' formation in both attack and defence. According to Brigadier-General Sir James Edmonds, the compiler of the official

histories of World War I, this change was made by the War
Cabinet against the advice of the Army Council and at a time
when there were 449,000 trained Category A men, over
nineteen years of age, in home depots, ready to proceed overseas. There is little doubt that the Cabinet had become
seriously alarmed at the heavy casualties in 1917, particularly
at Passchendaele, and that these measures were deliberately
taken to prevent what they regarded as unnecessary waste of
manpower in abortive offensive operations. These and other decisions were made against the advice of Sir William Robertson,
the Chief of the Imperial General Staff, and in mid-February he
was removed from his appointment and replaced by Sir Henry
Wilson.

It is not the purpose of this book to describe in detail the
German offensive, but only in so far as it affected the Allied
advance which followed in the summer and autumn, and
which brought about the Armistice.*

For the Germans the success of the campaign planned for the
spring of 1918 was vital. It was their last bid for victory while
the odds in their favour gave any hope of decisive results.
If it failed defeat would be inevitable. It is not surprising,
therefore, that the greatest attention was given to detail, and
every skill and device brought to play.

A feature of the operations was a new tactical doctrine. This
envisaged a short, but very violent, preliminary bombardment
in place of the long bombardments, often lasting for several
days, normally employed on the Western Front. This, in addition to conserving ammunition, made it much easier to attain
surprise. For the infantry a new attack formation, and method
of advance, was introduced. In place of the 'waves' of men
which had become customary, the Germans substituted an
advance in small widely spaced section groups (of six to ten men
each), echeloned in depth. This method had proved very
successful on the Eastern Front and was judged to be economi-
cal in manpower.

It should be noted that in the latter stages of the war these

---

* The narrative has been shortened by the inclusion of a comprehensive
map (Map 1) which should be studied when reading the rest of this chapter.

tactics—both for the artillery and infantry—were adopted by the Allies; and this infantry attack formation is still universally in use.

Although they were not planned initially that way the series of German attacks which followed consisted of five separate operations:

1. *Amiens*, commencing on 21st March.
2. *Lys*, commencing on 9th April.
3. *Chemin des Dames*, commencing on 27th May.
4. *Matz*, commencing on 9th June.
5. *Reims*, commencing on 15th July.

The extent of these offensives is shown on Map 1 and, as can be seen, the British bore the brunt of the attacks in the first instance on the Amiens and Lys fronts.

On the eve of the attack the British Order of Battle from north to south was as follows:

Second Army (Plumer)	23 miles	12 divisions and 388 heavy guns
First Army (Horne)	33 miles	14 divisions and 276 heavy guns
Third Army (Byng)	28 miles	14 divisions and 461 heavy guns
Fifth Army (Gough)	42 miles	12 divisions, 3 cavalry divisions and 515 heavy guns

In addition behind each army there were two divisions (three behind the Third Army) in general reserve under Haig.

Note. The Fourth Army did not at that time exist.

The first of these offensives against the British Fifth and Third armies met with spectacular success, as did the third against the French; but the other three were stoutly resisted and results fell far short of expectations.

To deal with the crisis which had developed a Conference of Allied leaders was held at Doullens on 26th March. It was at this Conference that General Foch was appointed Generalissimo of the Allied Armies, his duties being 'the strategic direction of operations, leaving each Commander-in-Chief in full control of the tactical action'.

By mid-July a very serious situation had been retrieved, and the last German offensive had shot its bolt.

For the Allies the price had been a heavy one. The loss of ground, although serious, was mostly offset by the awkward and vulnerable salients created in the German line of battle. The real loss for the British and French was thought to be in morale; but, as we shall see later, this was less serious than had been expected. The total British casualties from March to June were approximately 418,000 and the French for the same period 433,000. Those of the enemy are difficult to assess accurately, but have been estimated at about 895,000 for the period March to June and more than 196,000 in July.*

The material losses to the Allies were immense, as is always the case during an enforced retreat. In particular a large number of heavy guns were lost and great quantities of artillery ammunition of all kinds fell into enemy hands.

After the heavy losses, and prodigious efforts of both sides, during the four months from mid-March to mid-July, one might have expected a pause in operations. But it was not to be: with astonishing speed and resilience the Allied armies assumed the offensive.

---

* German official figures issued after the war are not regarded as reliable. The total of dead given for the whole war on all fronts is just under 2 million; but the 'Lists of Honour', giving names by regiments, show nearly double that number.

2

THE WESTERN FRONT IN THE SUMMER OF 1918

(SEE MAPS I, II, III)

Conditions at the End of the German Offensive

In the previous chapter it was explained how the great German offensive of the spring of 1918 met with spectacular success in its early stages, but failed in its aim of separating the British and French armies and seizing the Channel ports as a means of winning the war.

The losses on both sides had been immense; nearly a million British and French casualties being more than matched by the German losses. In material the Allies, being on the defensive, had been the heavier losers; but with the aid of ever-increasing American war production were in a better position to replace their losses.

In the early part of the year the Germans had the advantage in manpower as they were able gradually to transfer divisions from the now quiescent Eastern Front. By the summer the pendulum had swung the other way. The Germans had no prospects of further reinforcements, only casualties and wastage which could not be fully replaced. On the Allied side the British and French were little better off; but, on the other hand, American troops were now arriving in Europe in large numbers and would continue to do so up to a planned maximum of 80 divisions, which was the equivalent of about 150 British or French divisions—the American establishment being nearly twice that of her European Allies.

The Americans were, however, inexperienced and short of many items of heavy equipment. It was not expected that they could play a leading part in any offensive operations until the spring of 1919.

In these circumstances it is interesting to review the situation as it appeared to most people qualified to judge in mid-July 1918, when the German attacks were almost at an end and the Allied counter-offensive was about to start. The change-over by the Allies from the defensive to the offensive, and vice versa in the case of the Germans, was clear cut with no perceptible overlap. It came about during what has become known as the Second Battle of the Marne (15th July to 6th August 1918). The last enemy attack, to the east and west of Reims, began on the morning of 15th July: it made only moderate progress and by midday on the 17th it was evident that it had failed. At midnight orders were issued for the withdrawal from the small bridge-head gained over the Marne. Almost at the same time Pétain confirmed that the French counter-offensive, due to start on the 18th, would take place as planned. The Allied counter-attack ended in early August, with the withdrawal of the Germans behind the River Vesle.

Note. These operations are described in greater detail in Chapter 3.

The following statement shows the balance of opposing forces (by divisions) on 21st March 1918, when the German offensive

	ALLIES		GERMANY	
	21 March	*31 May*	*21 March*	*31 May*
American	4	4		
Belgian	12	12		
British	57	53 *		
French	99	103		
Portuguese	2	0		
Italian	0	2		
Totals	174	174	195	207 †

* Eight British divisions had been disbanded and four had joined from other theatres—a net loss of four.

† The increase in the German strength was due to divisions being brought from the Eastern Front.

began, and on 31st May, when the worst of the German onslaught was over.

The four American divisions were the only ones fully equipped, but there were many more American troops in France—infantry with their personal weapons, but without supporting arms. In a Memorandum dated 1st June 1918 General Foch indicated that 184,000 Americans had reached France in May and that he hoped the numbers would be 120,000 in June and another 200,000 in July. The aim was to have 48 operational divisions by the end of the year. Before the German offensive began arrangements had already been made for 72 American infantry battalions to be integrated within the British Army. On 28th March—seven days after the German attack began—the American Generals Pershing and Bliss placed the whole of their manpower resources in France at the disposal of General Foch in order to meet the common danger to the Allies. This was no small sacrifice, as the Americans had set their hearts on building up a great American army which would form and train in France and go into action as a unity, under American leadership. As Winston Churchill wrote later: 'This was an act of faith of the highest merit.'

In return the British Government—through Churchill, the Minister of Munitions—devoted their energies to providing the Americans with the artillery necessary to put their forces on a proper divisional basis. The Americans, aiming at 80 divisions, required some 12,000 guns of various kinds. United States factories could not provide more than about 600 of these in the required time; but by a co-ordinated effort it was arranged that practically the whole of the immense resources of British, French and Canadian armament factories producing guns should be turned over to equipping the American artillery.

To these material questions of manpower and equipment must be added the all-important one of morale. Since the outbreak of war the French Army had suffered two severe set-backs, both the result of abortive offensive operations. In the opening stages of the war the ill-conceived and reckless series of attacks against the German left wing had cost France very heavy losses. Up to the end of November 1914 her casualties amounted to approximately 854,000, about 454,000 being men killed or died of wounds or injuries. These were losses from which the French Army never fully recovered. Nearly three years later, in the Nivelle offensive of April 1917, France suffered casualties, in a period of nine days, which at the time were officially announced as 96,125. This figure was later disputed, and put at a total of about 187,000. There followed the very serious mutinies in the French Army which affected no less than 54 divisions out of a total of about 100. To these misfortunes was added the severe hammering suffered by the French during the 1918 German spring offensive. In these circumstances there were many people who considered it very unlikely that the French Army would be fit for a sustained major offensive in 1918.

The British Army had suffered very severe casualties on the Somme in 1916 and in 1917 in offensive operations in Flanders. Although these costly operations were severely criticized at the time, and still are, they had produced at least some tangible advantages, the main one being that of easing pressure on the French Army when its discipline was shaken and its fighting qualities at a low ebb. In the German attacks in March and April 1918 the British Army suffered heavily—much more so in proportion to its number of divisions than the French. Eight divisions had to be broken up and the Fifth Army was temporarily removed from the Order of Battle, its commander General Sir Hubert Gough being sent home.*

Nevertheless, in spite of all the derogatory remarks made in recent years about Haig and the First World War generals, the discipline of the British Army never wavered, and it very quickly recovered any temporary decline in morale.

It is to the lasting credit of the British Army and its leaders that it was the only army to fight from beginning to end in two world wars, and emerge victorious in both without any serious collective acts of ill-discipline.

Amongst British officers in France during July 1918 there was

---

* Later it was universally accepted that Gough had been made a scapegoat and unjustly dismissed. In 1937 some amend was made by the award to him of the G.C.B.

optimism and a general belief that, given adequate reinforcements, the troops were capable of early offensive action. It is, however, doubtful if this view went as far as an expectation of victory in 1918.

In the German Army there was undoubtedly some loss of morale, but there was no question of a general breakdown of discipline. By temperament the Germans and British are, in many ways, similar. Unlike the Latin races they are not unduly discouraged by failure or unduly elated by success. Moreover, in the eyes of the junior ranks in German units the spring offensive had not been unsuccessful. Large areas of territory had been captured and many prisoners and much booty had fallen into their hands. Only the heavy casualties cast a gloom. To the leaders things looked very different: they knew that, although they had gained some tactical successes, the operations had been a strategic failure. The war had not been won and henceforth conditions for Germany would become more and more unfavourable.

Although Germany's allies—Austria, Bulgaria and Turkey—showed signs of exhaustion there was, as yet, no indication that they were nearing collapse. They were, moreover, playing a very useful part, from Germany's point of view, by containing substantial Allied forces.

In spite of the relief felt in Allied quarters at the ultimate success of the defence on the Western Front, there were very few people who believed that victory could be won in 1918. It may be that Foch and Haig and a few others thought that there was just a chance of this happening, but with most it was no more than a hope.

No one can accuse Sir Winston Churchill of being a pessimist, but it is clear from two of our main sources of information that *he* thought the war would last until 1919. In volume iv of *The World Crisis 1911–1918* (Chapter XX, 'The Unfought Campaign') he explains how, in his capacity of Minister of Munitions, he planned a vast mechanical army for the decisive campaign of 1919. By 1st April 1919 there would be 3,629 of the Mark V and later varieties of heavy and medium tanks. These, together with French production and existing tanks, but allowing for casualties in the meantime, would, he calculated, produce by June 1919 a total of 7,166 heavy and medium tanks. In addition, there would be some 8,000 to 10,000 'little tanks' (Renaults).

Not all these would have been First Line tanks, of course, but in any case these numbers far exceed those used in any campaign in World War II. It is interesting to speculate on the date by which we would have been able to train the necessary crews for this vast Armada of mechanical vehicles, or if we could have evolved a satisfactory tactical doctrine for their employment—something which we had not succeeded in doing by the time we fought Rommel in the big tank battles in North Africa in 1941–42.

Another interesting item occurs in Haig's diary for Wednesday, 21st August 1918,* a paragraph of which reads as follows:

> Mr Winston Churchill (Minister of Munitions) came to see me about noon and stayed to lunch. He is most anxious to help us in every way, and is hurrying up the supply of '10 calibre-head' shells, gas, tanks, etc. His schemes are all timed for 'completion *next June*'. I told him we ought to do our utmost to get a decision this autumn. We are engaged in a 'wearing out battle' and are outlasting and beating the enemy. If we allow the enemy a period of quiet, he will recover and the 'wearing out' process must be recommenced. In reply I was told that the General Staff in London calculate that the decisive period of the war cannot arrive until next July.

This is interesting in confirming that opinion in Whitehall was that the war would continue into 1919. The timing of the entry in the diary is particularly enlightening. It was made thirteen days after the highly successful attack of 8th August, which was described by a German in the following terms:

> As the sun set on the battlefield on 8th August the greatest defeat which the German Army had suffered since the beginning of the war was an accomplished fact.

* *The Private Papers of Douglas Haig, 1914–1919*, edited by Robert Blake, page 324.

It is unlikely that Churchill, or any of the leaders in White-hall, would as yet be fully aware of the extent of the success of 8th August. They had seen too many early successes nipped in the bud to be optimistic so early in a new offensive. Haig, on the other hand, would know all the details and it may well be that it was at this very time that the conviction came to him that an autumn victory was attainable. There are also strong indications that it was at this time that Foch was similarly impressed by the possibility of a 1918 victory.

If further proof is needed of the way the Allied leaders—particularly in London—were thinking it is contained in a Memorandum of British Military Policy issued under the signature of General Sir Henry Wilson, the Chief of the Imperial General Staff, on 25th July 1918, in which he quotes an appreciation of what Allied and enemy strengths on the Western Front might be by 1st July 1919. It read as follows:

	Divisions	*Rifles*
British	44	400,000
French	65	461,000
Belgian	5	42,000
Portuguese	2	20,000
American	65	780,000
	181	1,703,000
German	170	1,230,000

To the Allied strength must be added the immense mechanical force previously mentioned as planned for 1919, which would have been mainly, but not entirely, British.

I think we can summarize this aspect of the matter by saying that in the period mid-July to mid-August 1918, both politicians and General Staff in London had very little belief in a successful end to the war before 1919; and that a similar view prevailed among French leaders. Before the successful attack on 8th August Haig had hoped for an autumn victory but doubted if it was possible. But the success of that attack, with its light casualties and indications of German decline, convinced him that, with luck, the war could be won before the winter. About the same time, or shortly after, Foch formed the same opinion.

There can be no certainty about this; but historically it is a point of great interest. It was the conviction, and whole-hearted enthusiasm of these two generals—the dour and aristocratic Scot and the volatile Frenchman of bourgeois origin—which imbued the Allied armies with the fighting spirit that carried them forward during the last three months of war.

We can conclude this brief summary of the situation by giving the Allied and German Orders of Battle as they stood at the 'turn of the tide' period at the end of July–early August.

The following statement shows the Allied Dispositions by Armies, with the German armies facing them. They are shown

| APPROXIMATE AREA | ARMIES | |
	Allied (29th July 1918)	German (1st August 1918)
Nieuport to just north of Ypres	Belgian	
	British: Second Fifth	Fourth
Arras	First	Sixth
East of Doullens	Third	Seventeenth
Amiens	Fourth	Second
Montdidier–Compiègne–Soissons	French: First Third	Eighteenth
Between the Rivers Oise and Marne	Tenth Sixth	Ninth Seventh
South of River Marne	Fifth	First
Châlons	Fourth	Third
Verdun to Swiss frontier near Belfort	Second Eighth Seventh	C Detachment Nineteenth A Detachment B Detachment

from north to south—from the sea near Nieuport to the Swiss frontier near Belfort.

Note. The line is that at the end of the German offensives as shown on Map 1.

STRENGTHS BY DIVISIONS

	Allies		*German*
Belgian	12		201
British	62	(includes 4 divisions with the French and 1 Portuguese division)	
French	103		
American	17	(2 more disembarking)	
Totals	194		201

Notes

(a) Of the 201 German divisions 74 were facing the Belgian and British armies and 127 the French Army. Of the German divisions 106 were judged unfit—that is, suitable for defence but unsuited for offensive operations.

(b) On 29th July several American divisions were with the British and French armies. Soon after this the First American Army was formed, and deployed in the Verdun area, on the right of the Fourth French Army. A Ninth French Army was also formed and deployed in the Reims area between the Fifth and Fourth French armies.

(c) On 29th July there were 54,224 American officers and 1,114,838 American enlisted men in France.

RIVAL PLANS FOR THE FUTURE

THE ALLIES' PLANS

It can be said that by 31st May the German spring offensive had lost its sting. Although the enemy was to continue his attacks for another six weeks the Allies had recovered their balance, and subsequent attacks met with dwindling success.

General Foch—whose pre-war writings show clearly how his whole military training and outlook were based on offensive action—began to lay his plans for counter-attack early in June. He aimed at resuming the offensive as soon as possible. It must not, however, be supposed that, at this stage, he contemplated a great strategic offensive which would drive the Germans eastwards and bring an early victory.

Foch's methods differed in one very important respect from those of Joffre. The latter aimed at attacking the flanks of the German bulge, between the Channel and Verdun, brought about by their occupation of Belgium and parts of northern and central France. This grand strategic conception would have produced big results if it had proved successful, but experience from 1915 to 1917 showed that success on this scale was unlikely. Surprise was virtually unobtainable, plans once made could not be easily changed and it involved attacking the enemy where he was strongest. It was a cumbersome strategy, lacking finesse.

Foch had different views. He believed in a series of less ambitious hammer-blows against small and vulnerable salients, or parts of the line where the German defences were weak. This method would keep the enemy guessing as to where the next blow would fall and, if an attack failed or progress was slower than expected, it could be halted and another effort made elsewhere. If success was attained at a number of places it was hoped that it would result in the whole front crumbling, and a general advance would be made possible. It was in accordance with this principle that the Allies passed to the offensive in the summer of 1918 and conducted operations into the autumn.

On 12th July Foch had requested Haig to prepare plans for an attack in the Béthune locality with a view to freeing the important coal-mines in that area. Haig was opposed to this on the grounds that the country was wet and open and, if the weather was bad, might be unsuitable for tanks. Instead he proposed an attack east and south-east of Amiens by the Fourth British and First French armies, so that this important town and centre of communications could be made safe. As early as mid-May Haig had directed General Rawlinson, the Fourth Army commander, to study such an operation in conjunction with General Debeney, the commander of the French First Army on his right. Planning was, therefore, well advanced. Foch agreed to this proposal.

Shortly after this, on 24th July, a conference attended by Foch, Haig and Pershing was held. At this Foch explained that he hoped to develop offensive operations in two stages:

Stage 1. To relieve certain communications which had been threatened by the recent German advances, and to attack any enemy salients which appeared specially vulnerable. By safeguarding places necessary to the Allies for supply purposes and straightening and shortening the battle-front these limited attacks were a necessary preliminary to more ambitious offensive operations.

Stage 2. Following Stage 1 to assume the offensive along the whole front by means of a series of attacks, with the object of using up enemy reserves, wearing down his powers of resistance and lowering his morale. This he hoped might lead to the disintegration of the German front; but whether or not he really believed this likely in 1918 is doubtful. It was probably not until a fortnight later—after the highly successful attack by Rawlinson's and Debeney's armies—that he became optimistic about an early victory.

At this same conference the following offensive operations were decided upon in order to implement Stage 1 of Foch's plan:

(*a*) An attack in the River Marne area in order to free the Paris–Verdun railway. (This was to be brought about by pressing home the French counter-offensive which had already started on 18th July.)

(*b*) To free the Paris–Amiens railway by the attack proposed by Haig.

(*c*) An attack on the Saint Mihiel salient by the Americans,* which would free the Verdun–Avricourt railway.

* The formation of the First American Army had been agreed upon on 24th July, but it was not completed until 30th August.

Beyond this Foch's plans were not revealed, except for the general statement that offensive operations would continue when and where opportunity offered.

Foch had placed Debeney's First French Army under Haig for the latter's proposed attack ((b) above). The essence of Haig's plan was secrecy, and most drastic methods were employed to prevent leakage. The right of the British Fourth Army and left of the French First were to break through on a wide front to a depth of five to seven miles. Thereafter Debeney's remaining corps were to attack in succession from left to right and later, if conditions were favourable, the French Third Army (on the right of the First) would join in.

(*Note.* This operation is described in detail in Chapter 3.)

THE GERMAN SITUATION

It is a surprise to students of World War I to find that the German intelligence was so inefficient. For a nation as well prepared as they were in 1914 it is astonishing how ill-informed they remained throughout the war. A quarter of a century later they were to prove equally inept in the intelligence field. This inefficiency is contrary to popular belief. Encouraged to some extent by their own Security Service the British people attributed almost magical powers to German intelligence. Spies were thought to be everywhere and capable of super-human feats of detection and disguise. In fact Germany was probably the worst served country of the major combatant powers as far as military intelligence was concerned.

Their assessment of the situation in the summer of 1918 was no exception to this general fallibility. An appreciation issued by the German General Staff on 2nd August stated that, whilst it was necessary to remain temporarily on the defensive, the offensive would be resumed as early as possible. It was considered that early Allied major attacks were most likely in the following areas:

(a) Kemmel—south of Ypres.
(b) Astride the River Oise.
(c) East of Reims.

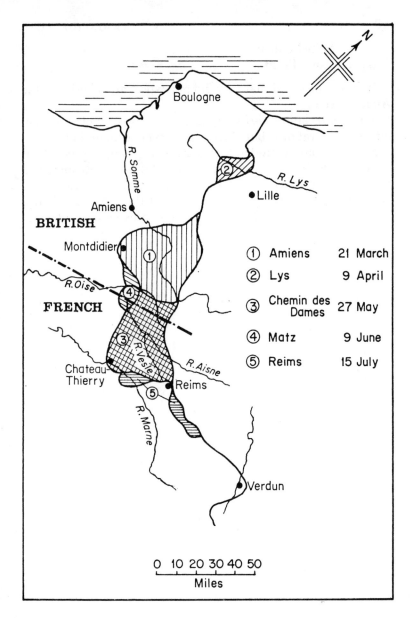

MAP I. The German Offensives, 1918

(*d*) St Mihiel Salient.
(*e*) Lorraine Front.

It should be noted that they did not expect an offensive in the Amiens Sector.

The appreciation also suggested areas for possible German offensive operations, but these were never to materialize.

So far we have considered only the background to the Allied offensive which was to bring about the Armistice. Readers will have been impressed by the fact that it was almost universally accepted that the war would go on until the summer of 1919. The chapters which follow describe how this view was belied.

3

THE TURN OF THE TIDE

(SEE MAPS II, III)

The Battles of Second Marne and Amiens, 15th July to 11th August 1918

For the story of the Allied resumption of the offensive we must begin by a brief description of the last German attack—the last act of their final bid for victory. It occurred on the River Marne, that same river which had been the scene of German misfortune in September 1914. It was here that von Kluck's and von Bülow's armies had been halted, separated and driven back forty-five miles to the Aisne, and Germany's design for a quick victory in the west frustrated.

The river which had seen the end of the beginning in 1914 was to see the beginning of the end nearly four years later.

At the end of June Allied intelligence was convinced that a further German attack was in preparation, but there were doubts as to whether it would take place in Flanders or farther south. General Gouraud's French Fourth Army to the east of Reims had captured prisoners whose interrogation indicated that attacks were to be made in Champagne on either side of Reims. This was substantiated visually when air reconnaissance revealed collections of craft for the passage of the Marne. The question was whether or not this was a blind to attract attention from preparations elsewhere. On 1st July Foch came to the conclusion that the preparations were genuine and he pointed out to Pétain and Haig that the enemy was only some thirty-six miles from Paris and Abbeville, and that an advance of twenty miles would be a serious matter for the Allies, and for the Germans offered results unobtainable on any other part of the front.

As further evidence of German intentions accumulated it was decided, on 4th July, to move French reserves to this area. In consequence a front which had been held by 17 divisions, plus 6 in reserve, was, under the new dispositions, held by 20 in front line and 12 (1 American) in reserve.

There then occurred one of those not infrequent differences of opinion between Foch and Haig. Foch requested that 2 British divisions, followed by another 6, should be sent to reinforce the French Fourth Army and that British offensives in the Béthune and Mount Kemmel areas should be prepared. In response to these requests the XXII Corps (Lieut.-General S. A. Godley) of 2 divisions was sent at once, followed by 2 more divisions later; but Haig protested about sending any more. He also disagreed with Foch about the offensive operations proposed; but in the meantime, on 15th July, the enemy, as predicted by Foch, opened his attack in the Marne area.

On the opening day of the Second Battle of the Marne (15th July 1918) the rival forces in the Champagne area were disposed as follows:

Allies

Holding the front from the Argonne (forty miles east of Reims) to Château-Thierry (thirty-five miles west of Reims) were, from right to left, the French Fourth and Fifth armies and half the Sixth Army—comprising in all 33 divisions, including 3 American and 2 Italian.

On the western side of the salient made by the German offensive in May was the rest of the French Sixth Army and the Tenth Army, amounting to 24 divisions of which 4 were American. This force was poised for the counter-attack timed by Pétain to start on 18th July.

To the south-west of Reims behind the French Fourth and Fifth armies was the French Ninth Army of 8 divisions and the British XXII Corps (51st and 62nd divisions in process of arriving). The Allied forces were supported by some 400 heavy guns and 360 field batteries.

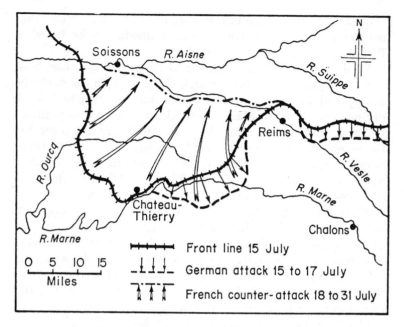

MAP II. The Second Battle of the Marne, July 1918

German

Opposing the Allied Armies on this front was a German force of 3½ armies, amounting to about 65 divisions.

The German artillery consisted of about 600 heavy guns and 1,050 field batteries.

The morning of 15th July was dull, but visibility was reasonably good. The German attack east of Reims was a complete failure. West of the city they met with some success, especially against the two Italian divisions who had to be relieved by Godley's XXII Corps, the troops marching into the line direct from their trains as they arrived. Farther west the Germans crossed the Marne and established a bridge-head some eight miles wide to a depth of about three miles. During the morning Pétain ordered the suspension of the preparations for the counter-attack timed for the 18th. It is a measure of Foch's

grip of the situation, and his resolve not to have his own plans
interfered with by the enemy, that immediately he heard of
Pétain's order he countermanded it.

By the evening of the 16th the German advance had been
halted: a French counter-attack on the 17th against the
bridgehead drove the enemy back some distance and his 6
divisions south of the Marne were left in a precarious position.

About midnight 17–18th July the order was given for the
Germans to evacuate the bridge-head. The last German
offensive had failed, and at about the same time as the German
withdrawal order was given, Pétain confirmed that the
counter-offensive would start on the 18th as planned.

The night of 18th–19th July was a rainy one, but at 4.30 a.m.
on the 18th the French artillery on the western flank of the
attack opened fire, followed at 5 a.m. by that on the eastern.
The bombardments were short and violent, and the attacking
infantry, supported in some cases by tanks, followed as soon as
it had lifted. On parts of the front surprise was complete, and
everywhere good progress was made.

On this very day Ludendorff was at Mons, where he held a
conference with German Army commanders and their staffs,
to fix the final details of Operation 'Hagen', an offensive
operation arranged to take place in Flanders. As a result of the
news from the Marne area most of the troop movements from
the forces in Champagne destined for 'Hagen' were cancelled,
and at the same time the withdrawal of troops from the Marne
bridgehead began.

It is interesting to compare this decision of Ludendorff with
that of Foch a few days earlier. Unlike his German adversary
the Frenchman was not to be diverted from his purpose by the
action of the enemy. It was Foch's strength of purpose, and
ability to make quick and accurate decisions of this kind, that
marks him as one of the great commanders of modern times.
This intensity of purpose was tempered with a flexibility of
mind which enabled him to take advice from others, and even
change his mind in face of convincing argument.

On the 19th the Allied advance was limited to two or three
miles on part of the front. The Germans defended themselves

with their customary courage and skill once they had recovered from the initial shock. Nevertheless, they recognized the situation as a critical one, and about midday they ordered a withdrawal from the salient to positions roughly on the line Reims–Soissons, behind the River Vesle. The Allies did little more than press the retreating enemy, except for a final effort on 1st August which met with considerable success in hustling what had otherwise been an orderly German withdrawal.

A surprising feature of the Second Marne Battle was the marked German air superiority. Although the Allies had available some 60 squadrons, enemy aircraft swarmed over the Allied lines by day, and bombed communications by night.

French casualties had been 95,165, and those of the 4 divisions of the British XXII Corps 16,552—a heavy toll for such a comparatively small force. German casualties were around 168,000, of whom 29,367 were prisoners: they also lost 793 guns and 3,723 machine guns. As a result of the battle the Germans were forced to disband 10 divisions.

On 6th August Foch was made a Marshal of France.

THE BATTLE OF AMIENS, 8TH TO 11TH AUGUST 1918

It can be said that the Second Battle of the Marne was the turning point of operations in 1918. It began with a German offensive and ended with a successful Allied counter-offensive. The Germans were never to regain the initiative on the Western Front. Henceforth they were either on the defensive or in retreat; the Allies on the offensive, advancing relentlessly eastwards towards Germany.

It was explained in Chapter 2 how Haig had persuaded Foch that a combined Franco-British offensive in the Amiens area was likely to pay a better dividend than one farther north in Flanders proposed by Foch. By the first week in August preparations for this operation were complete—the offensive that was to be known as the Battle of Amiens by the British and called the Battle of Montdidier by the French.

The troops involved were General Debeney's French First Army (under Haig's command) on the right and General

Rawlinson's British Fourth Army on the left, the whole on a front of some fifty miles from the Oise (Noyon) to the Ancre (Albert). An important feature of the plan was secrecy, and Rawlinson issued the most detailed instructions on this point. He informed the troops that surprise was vital for the success of the operation, and a notice inscribed 'Keep your Mouth Shut' was pasted in every man's 'small book'.

The outline plan for the offensive was as follows:

(*a*) The left Corps (the XXXI) of the French First Army, the Canadian Corps and the Australian Corps were to break through the German defences and, as their first major objective, advance to the old British line covering Amiens—an average distance of about six miles. They were not to delay on this position, but push on another seven miles or so to the German rear line of defence—using cavalry for the purpose if practicable.

(*b*) The French XXXI Corps was to start its attack forty-five minutes after the British: subsequently the remaining Corps of the French First Army—the IX, X and XXXV—were to advance *in succession* at intervals. The left of the British attack was to be protected by the British III Corps. It should be noted that the bulk of Debeney's First Army, by his decision to advance his Corps *in succession*, was in fact acting as a flank guard to the main attack by the British Fourth Army. This somewhat cautious procedure was hardly in accordance with the vigorous offensive action which Foch had ordered and expected.

The Order of Battle on the front to be attacked was as follows:

Allies

French First Army
  10 divisions in front line.
  4 divisions and 3 cavalry divisions in reserve.

British Fourth Army
  9 divisions in front line.
  6 divisions and 3 cavalry divisions in reserve.

The French had 826 heavy and medium guns (about one per 42 yards) and the British 684 (about one per 59 yards). The British mustered 342 fighting tanks and 72 'whippets' (light tanks); the French about 70 light tanks.

German

The front was covered by the German Eighteenth and Second armies, but the Second (14 divisions) had to withstand the brunt of the attack—from the French IX and XXXI Corps (7 divisions) and the British Fourth Army (15 divisions).

It should be noted that Foch had no specific General Reserve, except two French cavalry corps, the rest of his Reserve having been committed on the Marne. In reality he had about 77 national divisions which, although not directly under his hand, were available for his use if required. These consisted of divisions not holding the line; and comprised 10 American, 5 Belgian, 21 British, 38 French, 1 Portuguese and 2 Italian, of which about half were fresh and thoroughly battleworthy. Allied intelligence estimated the German reserves at about 60 divisions, many of them tired and all under strength.

The air situation was favourable for the Allies, as the French had about 1,100 aircraft and the British about 625 on airfields convenient for the front of attack. The Germans had only about 365 readily available, until more could be brought from Champagne where aircraft had been lavishly deployed for the Second Marne Battle.

The few days before the opening of the battle were full of incidents and not without anxiety for the Allies. The enemy fired large numbers of gas shells on back areas, causing over 500 casualties among units of the British III Corps. He also made a number of minor voluntary retirements. In retaliation for a raid made by the 5th Australian Division the Germans on 6th August made a raid against the III Corps and also gained some ground. This dislocated the Corps' carefully thought-out plans for the attack, by making it necessary to change the start line and the barrage programme.

The morning of 8th August, when the offensive was to start, was fine but misty, and at first visibility was little more

than ten yards in some places. Aircraft were not able to operate
until about 9 a.m. Nevertheless, punctually at 4.30 a.m., the
time set for zero hour, over 400 British tanks joined up with the
infantry and, as the barrage began, the assaulting troops moved
forward. The presence of mist cut both ways; it protected the
attackers from aimed fire, but caused them much confusion and
loss of direction.

Within two or three hours the mist had lifted. Not all had
worked out exactly according to plan; but on the whole the
attack had gone well. The forward defences were quickly
crushed, nearly 30,000 casualties (including 15,000 prisoners)
were inflicted and 400 guns and much other war material
captured. By nightfall the Germans had formed a new line by
utilizing 7 divisions from their reserve.

British casualties in personnel had been light—about 9,000;
but tank losses were exceptionally heavy, only about 145
remaining in serviceable condition. The Royal Air Force also
suffered heavy losses. It is of interest to record that among the
reinforcing German air squadrons, sent up from the front of the
Seventh Army, was one commanded by Captain Hermann
Goering.

The second day, the 10th, was a disappointing one, the
Allied advance being limited to a maximum of two miles on
part of the front. The confusion caused by the mist took time to
sort out and the problem of moving guns forward for the
further support of the assaulting troops proved difficult. But
perhaps the most potent cause was the state of training of the
troops, a factor which is usually overlooked when considering
the tactical problems of the last few weeks of the 1914–18 war.
For nearly four years the British and French armies had been
engaged in siege warfare, living a static existence in dug-outs
and elaborate trench systems. Such attacks as had been made
were mostly of a limited nature, carried out almost as a drill,
with very weighty artillery support and usually ample time for
preparation. Very little tactical skill had been required. Now
they were being directed against distant objectives, beyond the
areas of the trench systems, and demanding a degree of tactical
skill, individual initiative and quick decision which had not

been practised on the Western Front since the late summer and autumn of 1914. In these unfamiliar conditions it is not surprising that both commanders and troops were often hesitant and confused.

During the morning of the 10th Foch visited Haig's advanced headquarters, located in a train in a siding behind the front. He wished the attacks on the original front to continue in order to make crossings, and secure bridgeheads, over the Somme. Haig was not enthusiastic about this proposal, as he considered that an improvised assault against such a formidable obstacle as the River Somme was unlikely to succeed against the fresh German reserves now in position. He recommended an extension of the front of attack to the north on the fronts of the British Third and First armies with the object of turning the right flank of the enemy opposing Rawlinson's and Debeney's armies. Foch agreed to this, but still wanted the offensive on the original front to continue. In face of this Haig ordered Rawlinson and Debeney to continue their attack to the Somme and also instructed Byng (British Third Army) to probe the enemy on his front and advance as opportunity offered.

This incident was the first of a series of disagreements which ensued between Foch and Haig during the next few days— disagreements which were always expressed with tact and politeness, but were, nevertheless, very real. Apart from being poles apart in temperament, the two men also experienced considerable difficulty in communicating with each other: Foch could not speak English and Haig spoke French indifferently.

Very little progress was made on the 11th. Late that night Foch again visited Haig and, with some reason, complained of the inaction of the troops. He pleaded that the attack of the French First and British Fourth armies be continued and expressed the hope that the offensive of the British Third Army would not be long delayed.

But apparently the Marshal realized that his proposals could not be implemented at once, for on the following day, the 12th, he issued instructions in a somewhat different tone. He suggested probing attacks on the existing front in order to exploit the success to the full: this to include the capture of the important communication junction of Roye in the area of the French First Army. He also again pointed out the advantages to be gained by extending the areas of the offensive to the north, on the British Third Army front. Also to the south on the front of the French Tenth Army; but that army was not, of course, under Haig's command.

Except for minor operations the Battle of Amiens was at an end. There was to be a halt of eight days before the Allies returned to the offensive. British casualties were about 22,000 and French about 24,000. German losses were estimated at over 75,000, the British capturing 18,500 and the French 11,373 prisoners.

COMMENT ON OPERATIONS

The operations which had taken place between 15th July and 11th August were crucial. The Second Battle of the Marne had begun with a German offensive which had been only partially successful and ended with an Allied counter-offensive which had been a resounding victory. These operations, conducted almost entirely by French troops, indicated to Foch for the first time that the turn of the tide was at hand. It showed him clearly that the French Army, under Pétain, had regained its morale and was once again capable of offensive action. It showed that the German Army's power of resistance was on the wane.

These views were confirmed by the success of the Anglo-French attack which opened on 8th August—the Battle of Amiens—and convinced Foch that the time for an all-out offensive to finish the war had arrived. Haig had come to the same conclusion, although his methods differed from those of the Marshal. Haig had learnt a bitter lesson in 1917, particularly at Passchendaele, that once an attack had lost its momentum it was costly, and usually fruitless, to continue. Surprise had been forfeited and enemy reserves were quick to arrive. It was better to attack elsewhere at some point where the enemy least expected it. It may be said that Foch had the same theory; but from his more detached position he seems, at this stage of the war, to have been less able to judge when an

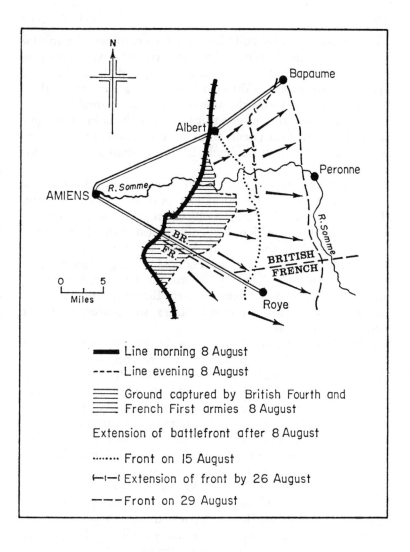

MAP III. The Battle of Amiens, August 1918

offensive had shot its bolt. His desire to continue the frontal
attack during the Battle of Amiens—when the Germans had
recovered and brought up fresh reserves, and the British and
French troops were still disorganized and unable to move their
heavy equipment forward fast enough—is an example.

It will not be out of place at this stage to give a brief account
of the reactions of the enemy to these events, and one cannot do
better than summarize Ludendorff's impressions as given in his
memoirs.*

On hearing of the events of 8th August Ludendorff sent a
staff officer to the battle front to report on conditions there.
He was deeply shocked by this officer's report, and records that
he was told stories 'which, I openly confess, I should not have
thought possible in the German Army'. He goes on to describe
how whole bodies of men surrendered to single troopers, or
isolated squadrons. Retiring troops meeting reinforcements
coming up had shouted remarks like 'Blackleg' and 'You are
prolonging the war'. In many places the officers had lost
control of their units.

Ludendorff attributed this very largely to the spirit of
insubordination which reinforcements recently arrived from
Germany had brought with them from their homes. He
continued: 'Our fighting power had suffered, even though the
great majority of divisions still fought heroically. The 8th of
August put the decline of that fighting power beyond all doubt.'

As soon as Ludendorff had confirmed these reports from
other sources, and generally taken stock of the situation, he
arranged for a conference with the Imperial Chancellor and the
Secretary of State for Foreign Affairs. This conference took
place at Spa—the German General Headquarters—on
13th and 14th August. Here he reviewed the military situation,
the condition of the army and Germany's allies and explained
that it was no longer possible to force the enemy to sue for peace
by an offensive. As this object could not be achieved by the
defensive 'the termination of the war would have to be brought
about by diplomacy'. That was on the 13th: on the following

* *My War Memories 1914–18*, by General Ludendorff, vol. ii, English
edition (1919).

day, at a meeting presided over by the Kaiser, Secretary of State von Hintze was instructed to open peace negotiations, if possible through the Queen of the Netherlands.

This gloomy view of the situation was not shared by all who attended the Spa Conference. Field-Marshal von Hindenburg pointed out that the front was still holding, that Germany still occupied almost the whole of Belgium and a large slice of France and that not a single Allied soldier stood on German soil except as a prisoner-of-war. This seems to have given a false impression among German leaders of the kind of peace terms they might expect, and that the Allies were likely to be conciliatory because of Germany's heavy losses and the brave effort she had made against heavy odds. It appears to have been thought possible to obtain terms which would include Germany's retention of a part of Belgian territory, including a strip of her coastline and the fortress of Liège. They had little knowledge of the feeling among the Allies, particularly Britain, who had gone to war in defence of Belgium and was in no mood to assuage the aggressor at her expense. Even Ludendorff seems to have thought that terms of this kind were attainable.

The conference appears to have been singularly quiet about conditions in Germany, which were giving considerable cause for anxiety: it was peace talk and anti-war propaganda, filtering through to the front from within the Fatherland, that was undermining the army and caused the 'regrettable incidents' which had come to Ludendorff's ears.

The attitude of the belligerents which followed the successful Allied attacks of 8th August may be summarized in this manner. In Germany a realization that military victory was now impossible and that an early peace must be secured by diplomatic means; but a much too optimistic view of the kind of peace that was attainable. Among the Allied military leaders on the Western Front—particularly Foch and Haig—there was now the belief that victory was attainable in 1918, although they did not, as yet, appreciate the extent of German deterioration at the front or at home. In London and Paris the politicians were still sceptical about the possibilities of victory before mid-1919.

4

EXTENSION OF THE BATTLE FRONT

Operations 20th August to 26th September 1918

(SEE MAP V)

In Chapter 2 it has been explained how Foch, in his general design for victory, divided the Allied offensive operations into two stages—Stage 1 being mainly for the purpose of straightening out the salients caused by the series of German attacks in the spring of 1918. The Allied attacks in the battles of the Marne and Amiens, described in Chapter 3, had opened the eyes of Foch and Haig to the possibilities of an early victory, but had not completed the battles for the salients. This chapter takes the story to the end of Stage 1 of Foch's strategic plan—up to 26th September.

In spite of Foch's pressure on Haig to continue the attacks of the French First and British Fourth armies without giving the enemy time to recover, little progress had been made after the successful initial attack, and by 11th August it had come to a standstill. In this respect it was much the same as all the offensives since 1915. The problem of maintaining the momentum of an attack, once the assault troops had outrun their artillery support, was still unsolved when opposed by resolute defenders—and the bulk of the German troops were still fighting bravely.

Foch had accepted this pause, but hoped that major offensive operations might recommence on 16th August; but the army commanders concerned in the original attack both demurred.

Debeney (French First Army) said that his artillery could not be ready by then, and Rawlinson (British Fourth Army) said that he was opposed to any hasty attempt on his front, which he considered might be a very costly affair without proper preparation.

On 12th August Byng (British Third Army on the left of the Fourth Army) reported that the Germans were withdrawing on part of his front, south of Arras. He was directed to follow them up vigorously.

Another difference of opinion arose at this juncture between Foch and Haig. The former could not agree that the resumption of the offensive on the fronts of the French First and British Fourth armies should await the major attack which Byng was preparing on the Third Army front for 20th or 21st August. The Marshal requested that 16th August be adhered to for the former operation, but on the evening of the 15th Haig went to Foch's headquarters and told him bluntly that he was unable to order an attack for the following day. Foch then informed Haig that as Debeney had only one day's supply of ammunition left for counter-battery purposes the attack must either take place on the 16th or be abandoned. As Haig remained adamant Foch agreed to cancellation.

It would seem that Foch got the impression, possibly correctly, that Haig was partly responsible for Debeney's lack of enthusiasm for a resumption of the offensive on his front, and he promptly removed the French First Army from Haig's command.

On 21st August the French Ninth Army was dissolved, its divisions being absorbed by other armies.

The battles which are about to be described began on 20th August and lasted for six weeks. They were designed to further Foch's plan—tempered by Haig's advice—of exhausting the enemy's reserves and lowering his morale by a series of hammer blows at unexpected places. They include the first major operation by American troops in an independent rôle—the assault on the Saint Mihiel Salient.

OPERATIONS FROM 20TH AUGUST TO 10TH SEPTEMBER

The series of Anglo-French operations which took place
during this period are known by a variety of names—the
battles of Bapaume (Allette to the French), Arras, Albert,
Scarpe and Drocourt–Quéant Line. As, however, they were all
of one design, and took place within the short space of three
weeks, they are best described as a whole.

During 20th–23rd August the French Tenth and Third
armies advanced some two miles towards St Quentin, but
were then held up by the German Ninth and Eighteenth
armies and remained practically stationary until the 29th.
The French First Army did not move.

Starting at 4.45 a.m. on the 23rd—supported by some 200
tanks and under cover of a barrage—the infantry of the British
Third Army advanced up to 4,000 yards on a front of eleven
miles, capturing more than 5,000 prisoners. The British
Fourth Army, which had started its attack on the previous day,
continued to advance and came up into line with the Third.
During these operations there were further signs of deteriorating
morale among the German infantry, some of whom put up very
little resistance. The numerous machine-gun detachments
were an exception: they never wavered and fought bravely
until the end of the war.

On the 24th and 25th the British Fourth and Third armies
continued to advance to a depth of about three miles, except
on the left of the Third, where they came up against the
Hindenburg Line. Preparations were then started for a deliberate assult on this formidable position.

On the 26th the front of attack was still further extended
when the British First Army, under General Horne, took the
offensive in the area north of Arras. On this day the Third
Army's progress was slow over difficult country still intersected
by the trench systems and general devastation of the old
Somme battlefields. But the First Army had a spectacular
success, advancing four miles. This had a salutary effect on the
German High Command, and Ludendorff ordered a withdrawal

of some ten miles between Noyon and Lens, a frontage of about fifty-five miles.

This retreat was soon followed by another farther north opposite the British Fifth and Second Armies—namely from the salient which had been won during the German offensive in the Lys area in April. For some days the Fifth Army had been probing the enemy defences in this area and made a few small advances. On the night of 29th–30th August the Germans made a deliberate withdrawal on this front, back to their original positions before the Lys offensive.

These withdrawals on the Somme and Lys were carried out with customary German skill and thoroughness. They were covered by heavy artillery fire, the use of mustard gas and extensive demolitions. The German Air Force was also increasingly active, especially by night.

During 27th–29th August slow but steady progress was made on the British front. The Fourth Army advanced about six miles, the First a little more than a mile. On the 29th the Third Army entered Bapaume. On the right of the British the French First Army also resumed the offensive.

These substantial advances on the British front led Foch to believe that the enemy was 'retiring in disorder', and he wrote to Haig exhorting him 'to continue the pursuit' with vigour without bothering too much about alignments or maintaining touch between formations and units. But Haig did not consider the time had yet come to take liberties. On a substantial part of the front the enemy had not been driven from his positions, but had carried out a methodical withdrawal—a fact which Foch seems to have overlooked. It is true that some enemy infantry units had surrendered prematurely, or fought with less than their usual determination, but the machine-gun teams and artillery, always the backbone of German defence, had not as yet shown signs of cracking. Whilst Haig agreed that the enemy should be pressed vigorously he did not agree that he was 'retiring in disorder', or that he was not still capable of offering determined resistance.

Further successes attended the Allied operations between 30th August and 3rd September. The right of the British

Fourth Army was held up on the banks of the Somme where the
river was a thousand yards wide and the approaches water-
logged. But below Péronne the Australians managed to cross
and then, by one of the finest feats of arms of the war, drove the
Germans off the Mont St Quentin position, a mile to the north
of Péronne. The left of the British Fourth Army and the whole
of the British Third then began to advance, and pushed forward
two or three miles.

On the evening of 2nd September the 1st and 4th Canadian
divisions, supported by some 60 tanks, broke through the
Drocourt–Quéant position. This success had the effect of
deciding the German Command to make another voluntary
withdrawal, this time a distance of about thirteen miles to the
Hindenburg Position, behind the Canal du Nord. This withdrawal was phased to take place on the nights of 2nd–3rd and
3rd–4th September. These successes had been gained against
considerably superior numbers—the British Fourth Army with
16 divisions against 33 and the British Third Army with 18
against about 33. But the success could not be exploited to the
full as Haig had no large reserve with which to relieve tired
divisions.

On 3rd September the British Third and First Armies
followed up the retreating enemy in true 'open warfare' style—
with advanced guards of all arms—in a manner which had not
been seen on the Western Front since the advance to the Marne
and Aisne in the early days of the war in 1914.

In the period 21st August to 3rd September British casualties
were about 89,500 and more than 46,000 prisoners had been
captured. German losses were estimated at about 115,600 men
and great quantities of material. The German official histories,
in reporting these losses, record that no reinforcements were
forthcoming and that the only way to maintain units at anything like proper strength was to disband some divisions and
distribute their personnel among others. Ten divisions were
disbanded in August.

The 4th September was a day of inactivity along the whole
Allied front; but on the 5th the British Fourth Army crossed the
Somme against weak opposition and made progress during the

FRICOURT. Mr Lloyd George (in front) with M. Thomas (France) and Lord Reading.

QUERRIEU CHÂTEAU. (Left to right) Field-Marshal Sir Douglas Haig, His Majesty King George V and Sir Henry Rawlinson (Comdr Fourth Army).

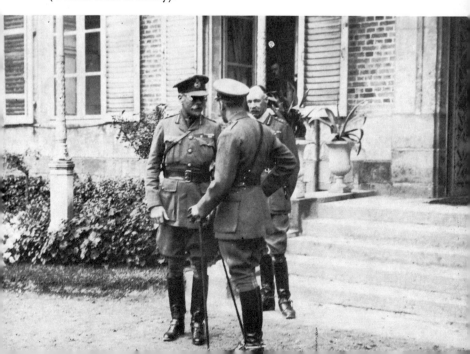

HAZEBROUCK, 15th April 1918. 48th Heavy Battery, R.G.A., in action beside a lane near Strazeele.

DOULLENS STATION. Field-Marshal Sir Douglas Haig conversing with M. Clemenceau, 13th April 1918.

next few days. The British Third and the French Third and First Armies also made some progress.

By about 10th September it had become apparent that the enemy had withdrawn as far as he intended to go voluntarily. Ahead of the Allies lay the formidable Hindenburg Position, consisting of advanced, main and reserve positions.

The events of the past few weeks had a depressing effect on the German High Command. At a conference on 6th September Hindenburg was very pessimistic about the outlook and doubt was expressed of the ability of the troops, in their present state, to offer effective resistance in the Hindenburg Position. Some senior officers advocated a retirement of nearly fifty miles to the Antwerp–Meuse Position, but this suggestion was discarded in favour of withdrawal, if the necessity arose, to another position some twenty miles to the rear.

THE ATTACK ON THE SAINT MIHIEL SALIENT, 12TH TO 14TH SEPTEMBER 1918

We must now turn our attention to the Americans, who had been arriving in France in increasing numbers during the spring and early summer, but whose participation on a scale commensurate with their manpower strength had been hampered by lack of heavy equipment, particularly artillery. It had been the American government's intention, and Pershing's hope, that the American troops would make their début in battle as a national army under their own leaders. This design had been delayed, partly by lack of equipment as mentioned above, but also by the seriousness of the military situation which arose as a result of the German offensive in the spring and early summer of 1918. With a commendable spirit of co-operation Pershing had agreed to American divisions, and in many instances individual units, going into action alongside British and French troops and under British and French command. As was to be expected, as soon as it was clear that the German offensive had shot its bolt, and the danger to the Allies was over, Pershing returned to his original plan of concentrating the American forces under his own command.

On 30th August 1918 the American First Army came into being, under Pershing, and took over the Saint Mihiel Salient position, to the south-east of Verdun. Pershing's immediate task was to eliminate this salient. His army consisted of 3 corps—the I Corps of 5 divisions, the IV Corps of 4 divisions and the V Corps of 3 divisions, with 4 divisions in army reserve. This gave a total of 16 American divisions to which was added the French II Colonial Corps of three divisions attached temporarily to the Americans for the operation. It must be remembered that American divisions were nearly twice as strong in personnel as those of their British and French Allies. Those familiar with equipment supply problems during, and since, the Second World War will be surprised to know that not one of the 3,000-odd guns which supported this operation was of American manufacture, and that of the 2,000 aircraft which participated 1,400 were British and 600 French. The French also provided some 265 light tanks.

Against this force the enemy mustered 14 divisions (one being Austrian), of which 5 were in reserve.

The American plan was to make the main attack on the southern face of the salient, this task being allotted to the American I and IV Corps. On the rest of the front there were to be holding attacks.

Early in September the Germans had decided on a policy of withdrawal from some of their more vulnerable salients, including that of Saint Mihiel. The American attack was launched in dense mist at 5 a.m. on 12th September, and it caught the enemy in the act of withdrawing. It met with complete success: American casualties were around 7,000; those of the enemy very much higher and including 15,000 prisoners and the loss of 450 guns.

Within less than forty-eight hours the Germans had lost the last of their salients on the Western Front, and American arms had won a resounding success in their first independent major action.

THE ASSAULT ON THE HINDENBURG POSITION,
12TH TO 26TH SEPTEMBER 1918

During this period the British Fourth and Third armies—opposed by 23 German divisions—gained a footing in the forward defences of the Hindenburg Position. Resistance was stubborn, and there were no spectacular successes. These operations were known officially as 'The Battle of Havrincourt' (Third Army) and 'The Battle of Epéhy' (Fourth Army). As the wings of these two attacks converged enemy resistance weakened, and better progress was made. On the 18th an enemy counter-attack by three divisions was beaten off by the Third Army and, as a result of this failure, the commander of the German Seventeenth Army (General von der Marwitz) was removed from his command.

The advances made by the British had so greatly reduced the frontages held by French troops that the French Sixth Army was withdrawn from the front line and transferred to Flanders, while the French Third Army was pulled out into reserve. That this redistribution of large French forces was possible was due to the predominant part played by the British armies in the fighting of the mid- and late summer.

Although British casualties had been heavy, they were light compared with those of former offensives. In 1916, on the Somme, there had been an average advance of eight miles on about a fourteen-mile front in four and a half months, at a cost of 420,000 British casualties. The progress made by the British between 8th August and 26th September, a period of fifty days, was an average of twenty-five miles on a forty-mile front at a cost of about 190,000 casualties. The total British casualties since 21st March (the opening date of the German offensive) were about 584,000, and during the same period they had taken 227,500 prisoners.

The difference in the progress made in the offensive operations just described, compared with that of earlier ones, was not due to any marked changes in the respective numerical strengths of the contestants. The main cause was war-weariness and decline in morale among the Germans. In the war of attrition the Allies came out best. There were, however, other important reasons—more artillery with more and better ammunition, better support from tanks and also improved tactical methods.

COMMENT ON OPERATIONS

The Allied offensive operations which terminated at the end of September 1918 brought to an end what can be appropriately called the Battles for the Salients—those comparatively minor salients which the Germans had made between March and June in the big salient created by their advance west nearly four years earlier. These operations ended Stage 1 of Foch's design for victory.

The Allied casualty figures given above show that the successes gained were no easy victories. Although German morale was weakening, it had not cracked. Among the ordinary infantry the decline was noticeable. There had been mass surrenders and cases of precipitate flight by large bodies—something which had not been seen before on the Western Front. But this decline was not found in all units and it was not found at all among the machine-gun teams.

It must be remembered that much of the ground gained by the Allies had been given up voluntarily by the Germans in their planned withdrawals. These withdrawals were carried out partly to spare their troops from impending attacks, and partly to shorten the front. By the summer of 1918 German manpower had dried up. There were no reinforcements left in the home depots to replace casualties and wastage: divisions had to be disbanded, and their units broken up, in order to provide reinforcements for those which were left. The British and French were little better off in this respect; but the flow of American troops to Europe, although they were not as yet fully effective, was something which, barring serious mistakes, was certain to bring an Allied victory in the end. This situation produced a feeling of hopelessness in the German Higher Command, which was gradually permeating down to the lower ranks.

It is not unfair to say that the big territorial gains of the Allies—mainly the British—gave Foch the impression that German morale was much worse, and decline in fighting efficiency greater, than was in fact the case. 'Retreating in disorder' was the phrase he used. The French retreat at Waterloo—when Napoleon's army was swept from the battlefield by the Allied advance and the survivors took to their heels and ran—was an example of 'retreating in disorder'. Nothing like that had happened on the Western Front by the end of September 1918, and in fact it never happened. Right to the end victories against the German Army were only to be won by hard fighting. In this matter Haig showed much better judgement than the French Marshal. Although the British Commander-in-Chief pressed the enemy hard—indeed much more so than the French—he continued to show a wise respect for German arms and did not incite his subordinates to hasty and irresponsible actions.

At this stage of the war Foch undoubtedly believed that Haig, Pétain and other senior Allied officers were too cautious; that they were still clinging to trench warfare methods and had not adapted their minds to the more open warfare which the Allied successes were bringing about. He considered it necessary to give frequent 'prods' to avoid throwing away fleeting chances of hustling the enemy. Most of these 'prods' were given verbally; probably in an informal manner which was well understood at the time, but which bears the stamp of recklessness and bad judgement when reduced to writing and read many years later. To this attitude Haig, very rightly, provided a corrective; but we must not blame Foch, or take his words too literally, for not wanting to miss any opportunity to rid his country of the invaders who had been there for four years.

Meanwhile conditions in Germany and in her army gave cause for the utmost gloom among German leaders.

In his first speech in the Reichstag, on 5th October, the new Chancellor, Prince Max of Baden,* was to express the view that Germany was still capable of continuing the war, and was

* Prince Max became Chancellor on 1st October 1918.

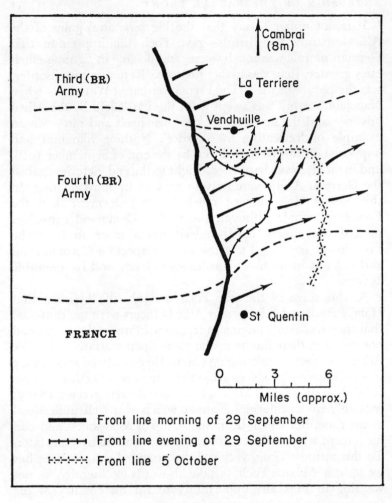

MAP IV

British Fourth Army, 29th September to 5th October 1918

This map shows, in diagrammatic form, how the British Fourth Army, by changing the direction of its attack northwards, helped the Third Army to advance and ultimately forced the Germans to withdraw on the whole British front.

prepared to do so if the Allied peace conditions were unacceptable. But these brave words were hardly in line with the views
of the military leaders, which were well expressed by Ludendorff in his war memoirs:

> Shirking at the front became more prevalent, especially
> among men returning from home leave. Overstaying of
> leave increased, and the fighting line got thinner and
> thinner.
> At home our attempt to improve the morale of the people
> by means of propaganda never got beyond the initial
> stages.

By the last days in September the German military leaders
had given up all hope of winning the war, and Hindenburg was
on the point of demanding that the government ask for an
immediate Armistice.

5

ADVANCE TO VICTORY

(SEE MAPS IV, V)

By the closing days of September 1918 Foch and his chief lieutenants—Haig, Pétain and Pershing—had become convinced that conditions existed which, with reasonable luck, could bring an Allied victory before winter weather on the Western Front put an end to large-scale operations. They do not, however, appear to have visualized the manner in which the Armistice would be brought about. They seem to have expected a disintegration of the German Army, a break or a number of breaks in the front, and a great round-up of German prisoners by massed cavalry formations which the British and French armies had both maintained for the purpose—but which were, in fact, never to be used on a grand scale.

In 1945 World War II ended in Europe with the complete disintegration of German forces. The great cities of the Fatherland were in ruins, the people were leaderless and law and order and the normal social services had broken down. The mechanized forces of Communist Russia from the east and the Anglo-American armies from the west poured into the country unopposed by any organized resistance. Nothing of this kind happened in 1918. The German Army had been greatly weakened: Crown Prince Ruprecht of Bavaria complained that the infantry of his Group of Armies had been reduced to an average of about 2,000 per division, against an establishment of about three times that number. His guns, he said, could not be moved for lack of horses to pull them, or fired because of grave shortages of ammunition. In addition to these manpower and material shortages there had been a sharp decline in morale—acts of ill-discipline in some fighting units and mutinies in rear areas. Nevertheless, the bulk of the German Army stood firm, obeying orders and maintaining discipline. No Allied attack was to make a hole which could not be repaired; there was no disintegration and no mass surrenders. The German Army was to stand fast on the agreed Armistice line and march home as a disciplined body under its own leaders—to the German people an army which had never been beaten.

In addition to the serious military situation, events on the home front and acts of ill-discipline in the Navy gave the German leaders cause for serious anxiety during the closing weeks of the war. This situation will be described in greater detail later. Here we will continue the story of the military operations.

The operations now planned by Foch were, to use a translation of his own words, for the purpose of 'employing all the Allied forces in convergent action'. They consisted of three separate offensives, from south to north (right to left) as follows:

Right

26th September, between the Meuse and Reims, by the American First Army (15 divisions) and the French Fourth Army (22 divisions).

Centre

Right Centre—on 29th September, between La Fère and Péronne, by the French First (14 divisions) and British Fourth (17 divisions) Armies.

Left Centre—on 27th September, between Péronne and Lens, by the British Third (15 divisions) and First (12 divisions) Armies.

Left

28th September, from Armentières to the sea, by the British Second Army (10 divisions), the Belgian Army (12 divisions), and the French Sixth Army (6 divisions).

The passive fronts were to be held as follows:

(a) *Between the Right and Right Centre offensives*, by the French Fifth and Tenth Armies (28 divisions).

(b) *Between the Left Centre and the Left*, by the British Fifth Army (9 divisions).

At this time an American Second Army was in process of formation to take up a position on the right of the First.

The total array for this final stage of operations was as follows:

Allies: 217 divisions of which 57 were in reserve. (French 102, British 60, American 39, Belgian 12, Italian 2, Portuguese 2.)

German: 197 divisions, about 113 being in front line and some 84 in reserve. All divisions were much below establishment and, at this time, the British Intelligence Service classified only 51 as 'fit'.

In spite of their successes in the earlier part of the year the Germans had found time and labour to improve their existing rear defences, and build other positions, against the day when they would find themselves on the defensive and perhaps fighting desperately to defend the Fatherland. Much of this work had been done by forced civilian labour in the occupied countries: all had been done with customary German skill and thoroughness.

The most important defensive work ran from Verdun in the south to the sea and consisted of the famous Hindenburg Position in the south, extended to the north along the Canal du Nord and in Flanders by the Wotan Position. The Hindenburg Position was particularly formidable—consisting of advanced, main and reserve lines—all with deep dug-outs and concrete machine-gun emplacements and protected by barbed wire. Behind this system of defence was another, the Hermann–Hunding–Brunhild Position, and behind that yet another, the Antwerp–Meuse Position and the frontier defences.

Apart from these extensive man-made works much of the country over which the Allies would advance was difficult terrain for military operations. In Flanders and the north the country was intersected by innumerable canals and rivers, and places like Lille and other industrial towns in northern France and Belgium favoured the defender rather than the attacker. Farther south, opposite the Americans, was the Argonne Forest, generally accepted by conventional military opinion as impenetrable and ruled out as an area for serious military operations.

There was no way round these defensive lines. Frontal attacks and stubborn fighting would be the order of the day. The question was—would the Allies have the necessary forces, the tactical skill and administrative support to advance over this difficult country and turn the enemy out of his strong positions; or would the Germans, weakened as they were, still have the strength and will to hold out and stave off defeat over another winter?

With this background we can now follow the operations leading up to the final phase just before the Armistice. This is best done by describing each of the three Allied offensives— Right, Centre and Left—separately, rather than attempting to describe the whole in strictly chronological sequence.

THE RIGHT OFFENSIVE: 26TH SEPTEMBER TO 3RD OCTOBER, THE ARGONNE

The first of the new attacks began with the French Fourth Army, under General Gouraud, on 26th September at 5.25 a.m., while it was still dark. That of the American First Army, under General Pershing, on the right began five minutes later. These attacks were preceded by an artillery bombardment lasting some 6½ hours and were supported by about 500 light tanks. The length of the bombardment and the noise of the tanks moving up destroyed the element of surprise, although the presence of American troops on part of the front seems to have been unknown to the Germans. A demonstration by the Americans east of the Meuse also mystified the enemy as to the exact limits of the front to be attacked. To meet this attack by 37 Allied divisions the Germans had 36 divisions, 24 in the line and 12 in reserve.

Good, although not spectacular, progress was made on the first day; the advance on most parts of the front being up to three miles, except in the Forest areas where, as was to be expected, less progress was made. On most sectors the attack penetrated deep enough to cause the enemy's heavy artillery to fall into Allied hands.

Tough fighting continued until 3rd October, and by then the advance in some areas amounted to about ten miles—again except in the Argonne Forest where it was less than half that distance. As the Allied troops approached the Brunhild Position much stiffer resistance was encountered, and little further progress was made until mid-October. This offensive served the very useful purpose of consuming a large number of German reserve divisions, 27 of which were drawn into the fight.

On 12th October a reorganization of American forces took place. The American Second Army (7 divisions) was formed under General Bullard, and came into position on the right of the American First Army, which now came under General Hunter Liggett. The two armies formed an Army Group under General Pershing.

THE CENTRE OFFENSIVES: 27TH SEPTEMBER TO 25TH OCTOBER, CAMBRAI AND ST QUENTIN

This great operation by the French First and British Fourth, Third and First Armies (from south to north in that order), between La Fère and Lens, covered a frontage of between fifty and sixty miles. On the British front—where the main attack took place and most progress was made—41 British divisions assaulted 27 German divisions in front line, backed by 14 more in immediate reserve.

The plan was for the British Third and First Armies to attack on 27th September and the British Fourth Army on the 29th; the latter protected on its right flank by the French First Army which was also to participate in the offensive. It was Haig's design that the main thrust should be made by the Fourth Army, and in accordance with this intention Rawlinson was given 10 of the 14 tank battalions allotted to armies, and also a higher proportion of a total of some 1,500 heavy guns and about 1,100 aircraft which were available.

On the 27th good progress was made, although the pace of the advance was not quite so fast as had been expected. By the afternoon of the 28th the British Third and First Armies had made a gap in the German defences some five miles wide. At 5.30 a.m. on the 29th the attack of the British Fourth Army began. On this front the most formidable obstacle was the Hindenburg Position, held by seven German divisions with another six in reserve. This was on the left on the front of the III British Corps. To the south the leading infantry of the IX British Corps swam the canal. On the left of IX Corps the Australian-American Corps (2nd, 3rd and 5th Australian and 27th and 30th American divisions), with the Americans leading, encountered stiff resistance.

By the end of the day an advance of over three miles had been made on the right of the Fourth Army, and practically the whole of the Hindenburg Line's Advanced Position, and about half the Main Position, had been captured.

On the same day (the 29th) the British Third and First Armies reached the St Quentin Canal and crossed it at a number of points.

Despite these satisfactory advances on the whole of the front of the Centre Offensive, the Germans were still fighting bravely and disputing every inch of ground. The progress of the Third Army (on the left of the Fourth) had been considerably slower than anticipated, and Rawlinson decided to widen the breach on his own (Fourth) Army front and then move north to help the Third Army. Substantial parts of both Advanced and Main positions of the Hindenburg Line were captured; but on the front of the French First Army very little impression was made on the Hindenburg Position. On 4th October the Fourth Army captured the Reserve, and last, line of the Hindenburg Position. On 8th October Cambrai was evacuated and the Germans fell back to the line of the River Selle, a distance of about nine miles.

These successes on the British Fourth Army front had exactly the effect that the Army Commander had expected. The enemy not only withdrew on Rawlinson's own army front, but also on those of the British Third and First Armies. They also retired on the Fifth Army front between Lens and Armentières, enabling that army to advance about ten miles to the Haute Deule Canal, almost without fighting.

With the capture of the last defences of the Hindenburg Position the British Fourth Army, with the French First Army on its right and the British Third Army on its left, moved on to the Selle, to which river the Germans had withdrawn. The British First Army was also able to come up into line and cross the Canal du Nord. As a result of these moves—mainly on the part of the British Fourth Army—the German armies of the centre (Third, First and Seventh) withdrew to the Hunding–Brunhild Position, thus enabling the French Fifth and Tenth Armies to push forward.

On 17th October the Fourth Army (with two attached American divisions playing an active part) crossed the Selle and captured Le Câteau, and during the following days advanced about five miles to the Sambre Canal. During the period 20th to 25th October the British Third and First Armies also moved forward. The successes on its flanks enabled the Fifth Army to advance unopposed.

During this period the French Fifth, Tenth and First Armies in the centre made small advances.

THE LEFT OFFENSIVE: 28TH SEPTEMBER TO 28TH OCTOBER, FLANDERS

The Group of Armies of Flanders comprised 10 British, 12 Belgian and 6 French divisions—a total of 28, opposed by 24 German divisions.

The offensive began on 28th September, in very bad weather; but in spite of this good progress was made, an advance of eight miles being made between Messines and Dixmude: the whole of the dominating Ypres Ridge was captured. The Germans in this sector showed a marked decline in fighting qualities.

The enemy withdrew to the strong 'Flanders Position'. Due to the continued heavy rain the roads became impassable in many areas. Transport conditions became extremely difficult, and it was not until the 14th October that the advance could be continued. It had been intended that the chief thrust should be made by the six French divisions, but their transport situation proved so difficult that General Plumer's British Second Army, south of the River Lys, made the main effort.

By 20th October the French and Belgians had reached the Lys. They did not go forward again until the 28th when the successes of the British Fourth, Third and First Armies enabled them to push on against weak resistance to the Schelde.

Thus the opening days of November 1918 found the five British armies roughly on a line from south to north as follows: a point east of Le Câteau just west of Valenciennes–Tournai–Oudenarde, in the order Fourth (Rawlinson), Third (Byng), First (Horne), Fifth (Birdwood), Second (Plumer). Since the end of September they had advanced an average distance of about thirty miles, often in bad weather, against the most formidable military field works ever constructed and against an enemy who was, for the most part, still fighting bravely.

On the left of the British was the Belgian Army, and on the right the French and American Armies whose advances had been slow after their initial successes.

THE CONTINUATION OF THE ADVANCE, 1ST NOVEMBER

On 1st November a general advance began, which was to continue until the Armistice eleven days later. On that day the Americans and the British Fourth, Third and First Armies resumed the offensive. The Germans continued to resist with their usual determination; but lack of numbers in their dwindling battalions and the heavy losses of equipment in recent weeks made their resistance less and less effective. However, the skill and resourcefulness of the machine-gun teams—combined with the fact that this weapon's comparative lightness made its capture less likely than that of heavier equipment—resulted in a steady stream of Allied casualties in these last days.

On the 1st the American First Army, assisted by the French Fourth Army, had a notable success. The French Fifth and Third Armies remained almost stationary, but the offensive of the British Third and First Armies resulted in the capture of Valenciennes and on the following day British troops crossed the River Rhonelle. These successes were followed by others— the forcing of the Sambre-Oise Canal by the British Fourth Army on the 4th, and the capture of Le Quesnoy by the British Third Army.

On the morning of 6th November the German High Command ordered a general withdrawal to the Meuse–Antwerp Position, that is the line Verdun–Sedan–Namur–Antwerp.

This brings the account of military operations to the point where an Armistice was imminent. Such further operations as took place will be described later, together with the political events, which may be said to have been part of the actual Armistice.

COMMENT ON OPERATIONS

It will be apparent from the description of operations that, although the Allies had been advancing steadily for three months, it had never, at any stage or at any place, been a walk-over victory. During that period, taking the whole front, the advance had been no more than an average of about sixty miles; a rate of considerably less than a mile per day. At no time was there a sufficient gap made in the enemy defences, or sufficient havoc caused on any part of the German front, to justify the unleashing of the considerable force of Allied cavalry waiting for the opportunity to deliver the *coup de grâce* in the classic manner. It is true that from 8th August onwards there were a few cases of large-scale German surrenders and others of men fighting with less spirit than usual; but these were never on a scale sufficient to cause disintegration on a wide front. In the majority of cases the German soldier fought heroically to the end. In spite of heavy artillery fire directed on his positions he had to be assaulted at close quarters with rifle, bayonet and bomb before it could be claimed that the position he held had been captured. Those who have visualized the

METEREN. Battles of the Lys, 16th April 1918. French armoured car supporting British troops (two companies 18th Middlesex Composite Force, XV Corps).

ST JEAN. Battles of the Lys. A picquet of the 10th Queen's behind a wire block on a road, 29th April 1918 (41st Division).

GERMAN HEADQUARTERS, SPA. The celebration of the thirtieth anniversary of the Kaiser's accession, 15th June 1918. (Left to right) Kaiser, staff officer, Field-Marshal von Hindenburg, Crown Prince.

BRUGES. The Kaiser (with fur collar) and members of his staff inspecting a captured British tank.

closing stages of World War I on the Western Front as a light-hearted chase after weary Germans who had given up the fight should correct their impressions.

The brief account of operations in this and previous chapters will have made clear that the main Allied effort came from the five British armies under Sir Douglas Haig. The French played a fine part, but many of their divisions had not fully recovered from the mutinies of 1917; indeed, considering the extent of those mutinies, it is remarkable that they had recovered so well. In detailed accounts of the fighting, and of the relationship of Foch with his subordinates, it is noticeable how often he complained of the lack of *élan* among French troops and urged them to be more aggressive. For newly blooded troops the Americans did extremely well and, in their early offensives, exceeded the expectations of their Allies; but their numbers were never sufficient to enable them to play a decisive part in the fighting. Their value was in their potential strength. German morale, particularly that of the High Command, was adversely influenced not only by the American soldiers in France, but even more by the tens of thousands who never crossed the Atlantic.

If the leading rôle was played by the British it is equally true to say that the British Fourth Army was the spearhead of the assault. It, together with the French First Army, delivered the blow on 8th August which, as a German writer put it, was '... the greatest defeat which the German Army had suffered since the beginning of the war'. In the final stage, reviewed in this chapter, the Fourth Army played the major rôle. Its success was largely due to the resourcefulness of its commander, Sir Henry Rawlinson. It was his decision to widen the gap made by his army and then turn north to help the Third Army, which was held up, that produced such a far-reaching influence on the battle. It was the Fourth Army whose men, on 4th October, captured the last of the Hindenburg defences and compelled the Germans to withdraw—not only on the front of the Fourth, but also on that of the Third and First Armies and eventually on that of the Fifth. This decision was a stroke of brilliance in the field of grand tactics the like of which had not been seen on the

Western Front since open warfare ended and trench warfare
began, in the early winter of 1914. Without this move it is
likely that the advance to victory would have been a much
slower, more cumbersome and more costly operation than it
was.

Haig's five Army Commanders—Horne (First), Plumer
(Second), Byng (Third), Rawlinson (Fourth) and Birdwood
(Fifth)—were all men with high professional qualifications and
with great experience of trench warfare as practised on the
Western Front. They were also men of high ideals and sterling
character as conceived at that time. But Rawlinson seems to
have possessed a sparkle, and a flexibility of mind, which
enabled him to grasp the difference between trench warfare
and the more open conditions of the last few weeks of the war
in a way which was lacking in most senior officers in the Allied
camp. 'Rawley' introduced a number of new tactical methods—
particularly as regards artillery support and co-operation
between infantry and tanks.

What manner of man was this commander of the British
Fourth Army who played such a conspicuous part in the
victory campaign of 1918? This is a convenient place for a brief
peep at his character. General Sir Henry Rawlinson is perhaps
best described as 'vivacious'—in a rather serious way. He was
a great talker and always prepared to join in a conversation on
any topic—a characteristic which was neither usual nor
fashionable among British senior officers of that period.
Although his military qualities were generally admired it
would be wrong to say that he was universally liked by his
contemporaries. He had commanded the ill-fated British
forces at Antwerp in 1914 and his 7th Division had been almost
wiped out at the First Battle of Ypres. Many people thought
him responsible for these disasters. Sir Winston Churchill, who
knew him well, wrote of him in his book *The World Crisis
1911–1918*: '. . . In the best of fortune or the worst, in the
most dangerous and hopeless position or on the crest of the
wave, he was always the same tough, cheery gentleman and
sportsman.' In 1918 you could not say better of a man than that.

In considering the undoubtedly fine feat of arms of the

Fourth and other British Armies, it is well to reflect on the probable influence of the offensive of the American First Army and the French Fourth Army which took place on 26th September between the Meuse and Reims (the Right Offensive). Although the advance was only a limited one it drew into the battle 27 German reserve divisions out of a total of about 84. This large drain on German reserves must have had a considerable influence on subsequent operations farther north. It would seem that this Franco-American attack alarmed the Germans out of all proportion to its actual importance. This was partly due to the appearance of American troops on part of the front of attack where they were not expected. The area was also strategically important, as a break-through or a substantial advance from that quarter could have out-flanked, and cut the communications of the whole German forces to the north. In the event the thick forest country of the Argonne made a rapid or deep advance impossible, but the Germans did not seem to realize this. The fact remains that one-third of the German reserve divisions were diverted to stem an attack on the southern flank which was never intended to produce decisive results.

In trench warfare conditions the question of supply had become a matter of routine. Every day the supply trains delivered their loads at the numerous railheads behind the front; every day they were collected from railheads and eventually transferred to unit transport (all horse-drawn), where they were conveyed to unit 'dumps' just behind the line and finally manhandled forward by unit ration parties for distribution to cooks or individuals according to the nature of the commodity. With food that was a daily procedure; with ammunition, clothing and other things it was on a weekly, fortnightly or 'as required' basis. Except in times of crisis, such as the German offensives in March and April 1918, this routine worked with meticulous precision. Occasionally it was interrupted by an air raid, shelling or exceptionally bad weather; but in conditions of static warfare these interruptions were invariably overcome and never caused a breakdown. The prospects of open warfare had long been contemplated—

indeed the aim of every offensive, from Neuve Chapelle (March 1915) and Loos (September 1915) to Passchendaele (October 1917), had been to get clear of the trenches and fight above ground instead of underground. Always the attempt had failed, until the expression 'open warfare' had become a joke with the fighting troops—a general's dream, a cry of 'wolf'.

It is, therefore, not untrue to say that these frequent frustrations resulted in the Allies being 'caught out' when in September and October conditions of at least semi-open warfare *did* actually come about. As the line rolled eastwards away from the established railheads, Allied road transport became severely strained, and in some cases—particularly among Belgian and French troops in Flanders—it broke down, and the speed of the advance was governed not by tactical considerations but by the limitation of transport. It is interesting to speculate on what might have happened if the Germans had made a big withdrawal, in one big leap, to some well-prepared defensive position and adopted a scorched earth policy towards the terrain left behind. This matter is dealt with in greater detail in Chapter 8.

6

POLITICAL AND
NAVAL CONSIDERATIONS

The Month of October 1918

As explained in Chapter 1 an Armistice is not a Peace Treaty, but an agreement for the cessation of hostilities pending a permanent peace settlement.

When we reflect on the Armistice of 1918 we are apt to think of it only as the instrument which ended the fighting by bringing about a cease-fire on the Western Front on 11th November. That is the popular conception; but it is not, of course, strictly correct. The fighting was brought to an end by more than one Armistice—with Bulgaria (29th September), Turkey (30th October) and Austria (4th November), as well as with Germany. Nor was the Armistice with Germany solely concerned with the Western Front cease-fire; other matters formed part of the agreement.

Nevertheless, Germany was the last of our enemies to stop fighting and by far the most formidable. The fighting on land far exceeded that on the sea and in the air in intensity, in the numbers involved and in the length of the casualty lists; and by 1918 the Western Front was the decisive battleground against the main enemy.

For all practical purposes, therefore, the Armistice of 1918 means the cease-fire between the Allies and Germany on the Western Front.

The four previous chapters have described briefly how the

Allies on the Western Front changed from the defensive to the offensive in July 1918 and then, by a series of hammer-blows, drove the German armies eastwards with the loss of vast numbers of prisoners and huge quantities of guns and much other war material. This land offensive by the Allies in France and Belgium was, without doubt, the main reason for Germany's asking for an Armistice and accepting the Allies' terms. But it was not the only reason: unrest at home, ill-discipline in the German Navy and defection among her allies also played an important part. Without the disturbances at home and in the Navy the German Army might well have been able to continue the war into 1919, with consequences which it is impossible to calculate.

The Armistice with Germany was brought about by a combination of military, naval and political events. The military events have already been described. To complete the picture we must now describe the other two, which took place concurrently with the great final battles on the Western Front.

On 1st October Prince Max of Baden became the German Chancellor. He was not a man of particular distinction, but was known to be of liberal views, was a quiet family man and his name had not been closely identified with Germany's war effort. In short he was a man likely to get a sympathetic hearing from the Allies in any negotiations for an Armistice or Peace.

It must be emphasized that some German leaders, even at this stage, had almost unbelievably optimistic views about the kind of Armistice and peace terms they could secure. In particular they believed that they might be allowed to retain a large slice of Belgium.

On 28th September Ludendorff had told Hindenburg that the military situation could only grow worse and worse, and that a request for an Armistice must be made at once. Further disasters on the Western Front occurred on the 29th and 30th, and on 1st October Hindenburg demanded that an immediate request for an Armistice be made. It was decided that Prince Max, the new Chancellor, should address the request to Woodrow Wilson, the President of the United States, and a note was dispatched on 4th October.

President Wilson had, in a speech on 8th January 1918, announced his celebrated 14 points as a basis for ending the war and securing a lasting peace; but these were more concerned with long-term events than with an immediate Armistice.*

On 8th October Wilson replied to the note, stating that evacuation of all invaded territories was essential before Armistice negotiations could begin. On the 12th Hindenburg and Ludendorff agreed to the evacuation of invaded territories. But Baron Ritter von Mann, the Imperial Navy Secretary, objected on the grounds that the submarine base at Emden and the naval base at Wilhelmshaven would be endangered if the Allies moved into the Schelde through Holland. Mann was, however, overruled and Wilson informed that Germany agreed to his condition. On this day (12th) an incident occurred which was to seriously stiffen Wilson's outlook. The passenger steamer *Leinster*, running between England and Ireland, was torpedoed without warning by a U-boat with the loss of 450 lives, among them some Americans. On the 14th Wilson demanded that German U-boats stop hostilities against passenger ships.

Up to this point Hindenburg and Ludendorff had supported the Chancellor's peace efforts with enthusiasm, but, now that it was becoming clear that Wilson's terms for an Armistice would be much tougher than had been expected, Ludendorff changed his views. On the morning of 17th October a very important meeting of the Privy Council took place at which the civilian members drafted twenty-one questions on military matters which were to form the basis for a conference with Ludendorff and Admiral Scheer, the Chief of the Naval Staff. This conference took place in the afternoon and appears to have been a very heated affair. The crux of the discussions was the last of the twenty-one questions: 'Will Germany be able to end the war next year on better terms than she can end it now?' To this Ludendorff replied that there could be nothing worse than the terms now offered by Wilson; but Prince Max disagreed and pointed out that the Allies could invade Germany and lay waste the country.

The conference then turned to naval matters, and Admiral

* President Wilson's 14 points are given in full in Appendix A.

Scheer was forced to admit that the navy had failed to fulfil
its promise to prevent the arrival of American troops in
Europe. Scheer, Hindenburg and Ludendorff were supported
by retired Admiral von Tirpitz in opposing the cessation of
submarine attacks on passenger ships. They took the view that
it would blunt the edge of the only offensive weapon Germany
had left. Prince Max was of the opinion that it would prejudice
the Armistice negotiations without bringing any significant
benefit. He also believed that the German people would not
fight in order to maintain U-boat warfare, which it was
generally believed had brought America into the war.

As a result of these deliberations Scheer, in private discussion
with the Kaiser, urged him to press the Chancellor to alter his
view; but, at a meeting between the Kaiser and Prince Max
on the 20th, the Kaiser bowed to the latter's view after he had
threatened to ask permission to resign.

These high-level talks and deliberations were soon followed
by disturbing happenings in the German Navy. On 21st
October—the day Wilson was informed of Germany's agreement to limit submarine warfare—Scheer ordered Vice-
Admiral von Hipper, Commander-in-Chief of the High Seas
Fleet, to make the fleet ready 'for attack and battle with the
English fleet'. This order was given without the knowledge of
either the Kaiser or Prince Max. Hipper approved and began
planning for an operation between the Flanders coast and the
Thames Estuary. It was to be a 'forlorn hope' battle to 'preserve
the honour of the German Navy'. By the 28th the fleet was to
be at Schillig Roads, near Wilhelmshaven, ready for action.

As if not to be outdone by his naval colleagues, Ludendorff
on 25th October—also without the Kaiser's knowledge—
published an Order of the Day declaring the Armistice terms
unacceptable. On the 27th the Kaiser informed Ludendorff
that he intended to consult two other generals about the land
war situation. Ludendorff at once asked permission to resign
and this was granted. Thereupon the man who had played so
great a part in shaping Germany's destinies left headquarters
and ceased to take any further part in public affairs. A similar
request to resign from Hindenburg was refused by the Kaiser.

Meanwhile, on 23rd October, a third note had been received by Berlin from President Wilson intimating that surrender, rather than negotiations, would be demanded if the Kaiser and his military advisers remained in power.

Ludendorff was succeeded by General Gröner from the Eastern Front. Meanwhile the Kaiser called into consultation Generals von Gallwitz, a Group of Armies commander, and Mudra, an Army Commander. They both gave a very pessimistic view of the situation, saying that the troops were exhausted and reinforcements non-existent. At the same time Gröner intimated that he saw no alternative to accepting an Armistice based on President Wilson's terms.

On the 29th another serious development took place in the German Navy. Many of the lower ranks had become aware of the purpose of the preparations being made for the fleet to put to sea, and considered that their lives were to be uselessly sacrificed against the more powerful British fleet in order to prevent the surrender of their ships to the Allies under an Armistice agreement. Many sailors failed to report for duty and some refused to obey orders. Hipper was forced to postpone the proposed operation, and it soon became apparent that it would have to be abandoned. Part of the fleet was sent to Kiel, where many of the men had their homes. This proved a serious mistake, as Kiel was a centre of discontent. What had started as a naval mutiny was to assume the guise of a revolution directed by the recently formed Workers' and Sailors' Soviet, an organization on the Russian model.

During these events the British and French governments had welcomed President Wilson's rôle as a negotiator, and had approved his preliminary condition that no detailed talks could take place until Germany agreed to evacuate occupied territory and restrict submarine warfare. There was, however, some anxiety in both Allied capitals that the President might make the Armistice agreement a political issue, whereas the British and French view, and certainly that of the Allied service chiefs, was that it was a military matter which should be left to Marshal Foch. In the event this view prevailed.

The story of World War I during the month of October 1918

is one of complicated political negotiations, great and decisive land battles, German naval mutinies and the threat of serious disturbances on the German home front. The Allies were attempting by every means to end the war in 1918: the German leaders were undecided until the last week as to whether it would be better to fight on or accept Armistice conditions which, surprisingly, some of them regarded as harsh.

It will help to clarify the picture if we consider the position as it appeared to the two sides on 1st November 1918.

THE ALLIES

Western Front. The Allied Armies, particularly on the British front, were rolling slowly forward towards Germany. In some cases the enemy was being driven from his positions; in others he was carrying out a planned withdrawal. The Allied advance was slow because of supply difficulties, demolitions, the bad conditions of the roads and enemy resistance against Allied troops who were unaccustomed to open warfare conditions. The advancing armies were also under an obligation to feed the civil population in the liberated areas. The Allies were still suffering casualties on a considerable scale, and were not fully aware of the German Army's lowering morale and its man-power problems. Largely due to the machine-gun teams and artillery the German Army, in Allied eyes, was still capable of maintaining an unbroken and solid front.

The Naval Situation. U-boat attacks on Allied shipping which had been such a serious aspect of the war in 1917 had been overcome by 1918. Allied and neutral merchant ships sunk in April 1917 had amounted to 850,000 tons, but had been reduced to 280,000 tons in August 1918 and to 120,000 tons by October 1918.

The British naval authorities were not unaware of the possibility of the German High Seas Fleet putting to sea for a 'forlorn hope' battle, and plans to meet such an eventuality had been made.

Armistice Negotiations. In reply to the German request for an Armistice President Wilson had stated that the terms of an eventual peace would have to be based on his 14 points, and that before any detailed Armistice conditions could be discussed the enemy must agree to abandon all invaded territory and cease U-boat action against passenger ships.

Two of Germany's allies—Bulgaria (on 29th September) and Turkey (on 30th October)—had already concluded cease-fire arrangements with the Allies and the third (Austria) was on the point of doing so.

GERMANY

Western Front. To the German leaders the situation on the Western Front probably appeared the most satisfactory item on a list of extremely gloomy prospects. The front remained intact despite the heavy losses in men and material and the continuous withdrawals. There were still some who thought it would be possible to hang on and continue the fight until the spring of 1919. This was not, however, the view of the subordinate commanders at the front, who saw only too clearly the shortage of men with no prospect of reinforcements, the lack of many types of ammunition, the lack of mobility through the shortage of horses and, above all, the decline in morale. This pessimism was undoubtedly increased by lack of appreciation of the Allies' troubles. If they could have seen the 'other side of the hill', and had a glimpse of the transport and supply difficulties on the Allied front, it might have relieved their anxiety to some extent. As it was they viewed the situation as one which could only get worse, and end in disaster if it continued much longer.

The Naval Situation. During the latter half of 1917 and in 1918 the Navy had become increasingly unpopular in Germany; firstly because unrestricted submarine warfare was regarded as the cause of America's entry into the war and secondly because of its failure to implement the promise to prevent American troops crossing the Atlantic. The mutinies at the end of October came as a profound shock to the Kaiser and other leaders, although they did not at first know what had sparked them off, the decision to take the fleet to sea having been a secret within the Navy Department. As the news of the mutinies became known among the general public it may well have caused satisfaction to many—who saw the Navy's ill-discipline as a step towards ending the war.

The Home Front. The first significant sign of discontent at home was the big strike of January 1918. Many deserters and men coming home on leave from the Eastern Front had been affected by Bolshevik ideas, and had spread them among the civil population. But the Germans are a well-disciplined and unemotional people, and until the late summer there had been a general belief in victory. There had been agitation among the Social Democrats, but this had hardly amounted to a threat of revolution. By the end of October the situation had changed. As the news of the naval mutinies and the defeats on the Western Front seeped through to the workers, unrest increased and became more open. There were widespread demands for peace. Prince Max, and even Hindenburg, came to the conclusion that there was a very real danger of revolution.

Armistice Negotiations. Since 1st October, when he became Chancellor, Prince Max had displayed a balance and sense of realities far superior to that shown by other German leaders, civil or military. He came to office among tired men who had spent four years directing the war, and his short period in the appointment—six weeks—is a good example of the value of a fresh brain on long-standing problems. He, more than any other German leader, realized that a cease-fire was essential under almost any conditions, and very early in his stewardship he took steps to bring it about. By the last day of October the stage was set for an early Armistice—Ludendorff had gone, and Hindenburg and the other generals whom the Kaiser had consulted were by then all convinced that the situation was desperate. President Wilson had made clear the general conditions for an Armistice and it was highly unlikely that anything in the detailed terms would make it unacceptable.

Thus by 1st November both sides were eager for an Armistice. The Allies because the military situation was highly satisfactory and they wished to avoid another winter campaign: the Germans because the only alternative appeared to be armed invasion, revolution and internal chaos.

7

THE ARMISTICE

(SEE MAP V)

The two previous chapters have brought the story to the opening days of November. On the Western Front the Germans —with their line of battle crumbling and bent, but still unbroken—had decided to withdraw to the Meuse–Antwerp Position (the line Verdun–Sedan–Namur–Antwerp). On the home front Germany's situation was critical: the Imperial Navy was in a state of mutiny and no longer a fighting force: the workers were in a condition of unrest bordering on revolution. In short, Germany was at the end of her tether.

In contrast the British and French, although their manpower was exhausted and their material resources in many ways at a low ebb, had undergone a remarkable revival of morale since the almost continuous advance on the Western Front had begun in August. Perhaps the deepest reason for Allied confidence was to be found in the expanding and almost limitless manpower, and other military resources, coming from America in an increasing flow. Moreover, these Americans had shown themselves to be good fighters.

The difference in the position of the two sides was that the Allies had good prospects of improving their position: Germany had none, only that things would get worse and worse. In these circumstances both were anxious for a cease-fire; but the Allies only on their own terms; the Germans on almost any terms.

75

It will have become apparent that the events leading up to the Armistice had begun with the failure of the series of German spring and summer offensives to produce decisive results, and the turn of the tide in favour of the Allies in July and August. After that Germany's situation rapidly declined and the Allies' position improved. But, as has been explained, Allied statesmen—particularly in Britain—were slow to believe that the war could be won in 1918.

By 1st November even the doubters in the Allied camp had been converted. An Armistice in the near future was firmly in sight: to most people, on both sides of the firing line, it was now only a question of the terms and the exact date. In this chapter the final act of the shooting war—the Armistice—is described.

POLITICAL MOVES

During the last week in October the German Imperial Chancellor, Prince Max, was attacked by a particularly virulent type of influenza which had swept across Europe and most of Asia in 1918. By the time he returned to full duty on 4th November Bulgaria, Turkey and Austria had all negotiated Armistice terms with the Allies; and in other respects the situation for Germany appeared to be desperate.

On 6th November Ludendorff's successor, Gröner, informed the Chancellor that an Armistice must be negotiated by the 9th at the latest. About this time a number of mutinies broke out in the German Army, and demonstrations on the lines of communication by absentees took place. In isolation no incident was very serious, but cumulatively they created a dismal impression in Spa and Berlin.

On the evening of the 6th the Allied governments told Berlin by wireless that Marshal Foch had been authorized to receive representatives of the German Government and to inform them of the terms on which an Armistice would be granted. The German Armistice delegation crossed the front line on the night of 7–8th November.

On the 8th some thirty senior German officers from the Western Front were summoned to Spa and were asked if they considered that the Army could be relied upon to suppress a revolution. To this question their answer was 'No'—unanimously it is believed. This incident seems to have been the final act which dictated the events of the next few days.

At 2 p.m. on 9th November a republic was proclaimed in Berlin for the whole of Germany, and Herr Ebert took over the Chancellorship from Prince Max. The only senior member left of the Kaiser's old advisers was Hindenburg and, on the latter's advice, William II left Spa for Holland during the early hours of 10th November.

MILITARY OPERATIONS—THE FINAL PHASE

By the first week in November winter weather had started, and during the last few days of the war (5th to 11th November) rain fell almost continuously. As the Allies' advance continued they found the roads in bad condition and churned with mud: movement off the roads was rarely possible. These conditions, combined with enemy demolitions and supply difficulties, inevitably slowed up the Allied advance, even on parts of the front where German resistance was weak or non-existent.

In outline the course of events, from north to south, was as follows:

THE GROUP OF ARMIES OF FLANDERS
(BELGIAN ARMY, FRENCH SIXTH ARMY AND THE BRITISH FIFTH AND SECOND ARMIES)

Progress on this front was slight until the 8th as the troops were held up on the Schelde, but on that date the Germans retired; the Allies then crossed without opposition and continued the pursuit.

THE CENTRE FRONT
(FRENCH FOURTH AND THIRD AND BRITISH FOURTH, THIRD AND FIRST ARMIES)

Here steady progress was made against German rearguards who destroyed bridges and systematically cratered the roads. These rearguards consisted almost entirely of artillery and machine-gun teams.

THE RIGHT FRONT

The American First Army was heavily engaged as it not only crossed the Meuse but drove the enemy from some high ground (Hauts de Meuse) east of the river.

In these last days the pattern of the fighting was more like the open warfare visualized in pre-1914 military textbooks than it had been since the early weeks on the Western Front in 1914.* Little help was given by the Allied Air Forces, as the weather was unsuitable for flying.

Soon after midday on 9th November the British Guards Division occupied the fortress of Maubeuge, and that afternoon Marshal Foch sent the following message to his three Commanders-in-Chief—Haig, Pétain and Pershing:

> The enemy disorganized by our repeated attacks is yielding ground on the whole front. Our advance should be kept going and speeded up. I appeal to the energy and initiative of the Commanders-in-Chief to make the results obtained decisive.

In the spirit of this order the advance guards pressed forward along the whole front; but owing to the conditions already described progress was nowhere spectacular, and in these final days very few prisoners were taken. An advance of about eight miles was the maximum.

On 10th November—a very bad day with fog in many areas —the same procedure was adopted. At Mons, where the B.E.F. had received its baptism of fire in 1914, the enemy resisted desperately, and it was not until dawn on the following day that the Canadian Corps captured the town.

On 11th November the following message, timed 6.50 a.m., was sent out from Haig's headquarters, and similar messages were sent from other headquarters:

> Hostilities will cease at 11.00 hours today, November 11th. Troops will stand fast on the line reached at that hour, which will be reported by wire to Advanced G.H.Q.

* For a more detailed account of the tactical methods employed see Chapter 8.

Defensive precautions will be maintained. There will be no intercourse of any description with the enemy until receipt of instructions from G.H.Q. Further instructions follow.

Between 9 a.m. and 10 a.m. the following more detailed instructions were issued to armies:

1. Our own troops will not advance east of a line gained by them when hostilities ceased. Our aeroplanes will keep a distance of not less than a mile behind this line except for the purpose of driving back hostile aeroplanes as indicated in paragraph 3.

2. There is to be no unauthorized intercourse or fraternization of any description with enemy. He will not be permitted to approach our lines and any attempt to do so will be immediately stopped, if necessary by fire. Any parties of enemy coming over our lines under a white flag will be made prisoners and the fact reported.

3. No enemy aircraft will be permitted to cross the line. Should any make the attempt to do so they will be attacked by fire from ground and from air.

4. All commanders are to pay strictest attention to discipline, smartness and well-being of their troops, so as to ensure highest state of efficiency being maintained throughout British forces. Troops will be given every opportunity for rest, training, recreation and leave.

5. Passage of civilians through our lines in either direction will be regulated in accordance with instructions which will be issued separately. In the meantime no civilians will be permitted to pass in either direction.

So at the eleventh hour, of the 11th day, of the 11th month of the year 1918, after more than four years of continuous fighting, hostilities on the main battlefront of the greatest war in history came to an end. The approximate halt line was Belfort–Verdun–Sedan–Maubeuge–Mons–Ghent (*see* Map v).

As far as British troops were concerned the arrival of eleven o'clock was taken calmly—just 'all in the day's work'. There was little cheering or outward sign of emotion. After dark this attitude was relaxed on many parts of the front: flares and star shells were fired, bonfires were lit and there was general rejoicing.

SIGNING THE ARMISTICE AGREEMENT

The actual signing of the Armistice agreement is of historical interest and merits a brief description.

The Allies were represented by Marshal Foch and the British Admiral Sir Rosslyn Wemyss. The German delegation was headed by Herr Erzberger, with Count von Oberndorff, Major-General von Winterfeldt and Captain Vanselow (German Navy) as members. General Gundell was originally selected to lead the delegation, but was replaced by Erzberger at the last minute. It is generally supposed that the change to a civilian leader was made at Hindenburg's instigation to avoid the stigma of surrender falling too heavily on the German Army. This may have been a partial reason for the change, but it seems likely that the chief consideration was the intimation in President Wilson's third note that the Allies were not prepared to negotiate with the Kaiser or any of his military advisers. In these circumstances a civilian head of the delegation would be preferable to one headed by a senior member of the General Staff.

Leaving Berlin on 6th November the German delegation crossed the front line on the night of 7th–8th and was conducted to Marshal Foch's headquarters in a train in the Compiègne Forest, near Rétondes,* where they arrived at about 7 a.m. on the 8th.

Accounts of the first meeting with Foch differ in detail; but, after some preliminary passages, Foch intimated that he was not prepared to discuss terms but was there to inform the Germans of the conditions under which they could obtain a cease-fire. General Weygand,† his Chief of Staff, then read out the Armistice terms.

* Nearly twenty-two years later, on 21st June 1940, Hitler, with his penchant for the dramatic, caused the German-dictated Armistice with France to be signed in the same railway coach at the same place.

† General Weygand will be remembered as the man who succeeded General Gamelin in command of the French forces in France in May 1940 in a last, but unsuccessful, attempt to retrieve the situation caused by the German successes.

The terms had been drawn up with the object of making it impossible for Germany to recommence hostilities once they had been implemented. They included:

(a) The immediate evacuation of all occupied territory, including Alsace-Lorraine.

(b) The evacuation of the west bank of the Rhine by German forces and the handing over to Allied troops of certain bridgeheads on the east bank.

(c) Repatriation of all Allied prisoners, without immediate reciprocal treatment for German prisoners in Allied hands.

(d) The immediate surrender of:
    5,000 guns (2,500 heavy and 2,500 field),
    25,000 machine-guns,
    3,000 mortars,
    1,700 aeroplanes,
    all German submarines.
The internment in British ports of:
    6 battle-cruisers,
    10 battleships,
    8 light cruisers,
    50 destroyers.*

The German delegates affected to be stunned by the severity of these terms, and endeavoured to obtain some amelioration. In his memoirs Erzberger states that prior to leaving Berlin he was instructed to accept any conditions, even unconditional surrender. This instruction was confirmed by two telegrams sent from Berlin to the delegation leader after the German party had arrived at Foch's headquarters—one from Hindenburg and one from the Chancellor, both authorizing him to accept the Armistice terms as submitted. The agreement was signed at 5.5 a.m. on 11th November.

Although at first sight the conditions seem almost as severe as it was humanly possible to devise, many Germans—the

* The full text of the Armistice agreement is given in Appendix B.

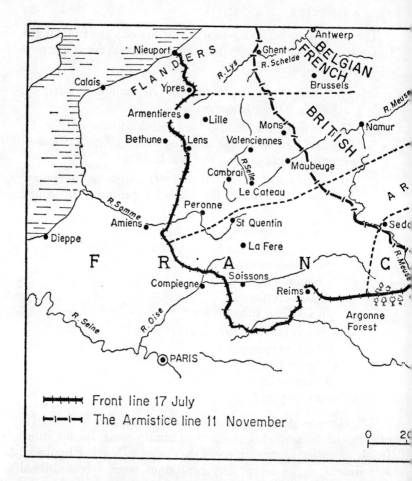

Front line 17 July
The Armistice line 11 November

0 20

General Staff in particular—were well pleased. The Allies
might have occupied Berlin and other big cities of Germany:
they might have demanded the surrender of all German forces,
deprived the soldiers of their personal arms and sent them home
as ex-prisoners of war; or they might have kept them in France
and Belgium as 'slave labourers', as the Germans had done in
some countries they occupied. As it was, the German Army
marched home in formed units with bands playing and carrying
their personal arms. The German claim that their army was

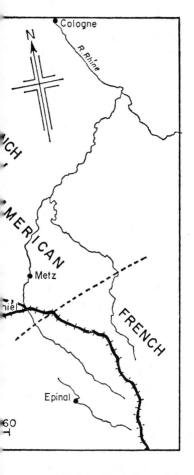

MAP V

The Allied advance to victory, July to November 1918

never decisively defeated is perfectly true. In spite of the great strain imposed upon it the Western Front was unbroken. How long it would have remained so is a matter for speculation.

The prestige of the German Army remained high in Germany after the Armistice, and it was able to perpetuate the partial truth that it was stabbed in the back from the home front. It was largely owing to this continued high prestige that the Army was able to re-form so quickly under Hitler. Less than twenty-two years after the signing of the Armistice of 1918 a new

German Army was to sweep to victory over a large slice of
Europe. Although materially it had been modernized and
mechanized, Hitler's army was founded on the old traditions—
and one of those traditions was that it had never been beaten
in the 1914–1918 war.

FLIGHT TO HOLLAND AND ABDICATION OF THE KAISER

In Germany at war the centre of gravity was the Emperor—the
Kaiser, the Supreme War Lord—to whom every German
fighting man owed personal allegiance, and to whose patronage
the Officer Corps owed its unique position. In the Allied
countries the Kaiser was regarded as the man who had started
the war or, in the light of more recent knowledge, the man who
might have prevented it, but took no positive steps to do so.

The manner of the Kaiser's flight to Holland, and his
subsequent abdication, was as dramatic as it was inevitable in
view of Germany's position in early November 1918. (The
flight and the abdication were not simultaneous: the formal
abdication took place more than a fortnight later.)

The Kaiser left Spa at 5 a.m. on 10th November—some
fifteen hours after Germany had been declared a republic. At
about 7 a.m. a small convoy of less than a dozen cars arrived at
the village of Eysden on the Dutch frontier. It is not difficult to
imagine the surprise of the Dutch police officer at the barrier
when confronted by this convoy and its uniformed occupants.
He refused to remove the barrier, but, after about an hour, he
was joined by a Major Van Dyl who quickly recognized the
Kaiser and guessed the reason for the party's presence. After
a short discussion the Kaiser and his companions entered
Holland on foot and were escorted to the nearby railway
station. Later the royal train arrived at the station and the
party entered it.

Meanwhile Van Dyl had caused the Dutch Government to be
informed of the arrival of the unwelcome visitors. It happened
that living at Amerongen, a little north of Utrecht, was Count
Godard Bentinck to whom the Kaiser appealed for temporary
sanctuary—on the grounds that they were both Knights of the

Order of St John, and that the vows of the Order made it incumbent on the Count to acquiesce to this request. On being informed that the Kaiser's party was more than twenty strong, and might reach as high as thirty, Count Bentinck somewhat naturally hesitated. However, following representations from the Government of the Netherlands the Count very soon agreed, and during the afternoon of the following day (the 11th) the royal train moved to a station near the Count's residence. The Kaiser and a few others were installed in the house, and the rest of the party in other accommodation. Later the Kaiserin arrived.

On 28th November a delegation arrived from Berlin. Its leader, Count Ernst von Rantzau, invited the Kaiser to sign an instrument of abdication of which the following is a translation:

> I hencewith renounce for all time my right to the Crown of Prussia, and to the German Imperial Crown connected therewith. In doing so I release all officials of the German Reich and Prussia, all officers, non-commissioned officers and men of the Navy, the Prussian Army and the troops of Federal contingents from their oath of allegiance which they have sworn to me as their Emperor, King and Supreme Commander. Until the institution of a new order in Germany, I expect them to assist the holders of the actual power in Germany to protect the German people from the dangers threatening through anarchy, famine and foreign rule.

No doubt William had been expecting something of this kind and had made up his mind. He signed the document without hesitation and he and the royal German family passed into obscurity as private citizens.

The ex-Kaiser was fifty-nine years of age at the time of his abdication. Subsequently he moved to the Castle of Doorn, where he lived in retirement until his death in June 1941. At the time there was much indignation in Britain and other Allied countries that he was not brought to trial; but, viewing the matter dispassionately in retrospect, it is probable that the Queen and Government of the Netherlands showed both wisdom and courage in refusing to comply with Allied requests for his surrender. Their hospitality to the ex-Kaiser did not, however, save the Dutch from invasion and occupation in 1940, at the hands of one of William's successors as head of the German State.

The Kaiser was more fortunate than many deposed monarchs. He did not suffer a violent death or even the vilification of his countrymen; he was not pursued or harassed as a refugee or outcast. Up to the very last hours this man, in whose name so much harm had been done, enjoyed the prestige and luxury of a sovereign's court and, on entering Holland, was accorded comfortable hospitality for the remaining twenty-three years of his life.

THE RECKONING

This is perhaps a suitable place to quote a few statistics in connection with what was probably the greatest folly ever committed by mankind. For four years and ninety-nine days the efforts of most of the great nations of the world were devoted to slaughtering or maiming the best of a generation of young men. The war not only dealt Europe—the cradle of modern civilization—a blow from which she has never fully recovered, it also created conditions for another world war twenty-one years later. Together they have resulted in the end of white European supremacy and leadership in world affairs.

GERMAN PRISONERS AND CAPTURED GUNS, JULY TO NOVEMBER 1918

During the Allied offensives, which had begun on 18th July and ended with the Armistice on 11th November 1918, some 385,000 Germans and over 6,600 guns were captured—the distribution being as follows:

	Prisoners	Guns
British Armies	188,700	2,840
French Armies	139,000	1,880
American Armies	43,300	1,421
Belgian Army	14,500	474

These figures leave little doubt that the men under Douglas

Haig's command played the major part in bringing the war
to an end in 1918.

BRITISH EMPIRE CASUALTIES, AUGUST TO NOVEMBER 1918

British Empire casualties (killed, wounded and missing) on the
Western Front in the infantry, cavalry, Tank Corps and
Machine-Gun Corps during the period of the final offensives—
7th August to 11th November—were approximately as follows:

Officers	14,768
Other ranks	299,438

Of these the vast majority were in the infantry.

WAR CASUALTIES 1914–1918

British Empire

Combatants who lost their lives	996,230
Merchant and fishing fleet seamen who lost their lives	15,313
Combatants wounded	2,289,860

Notes

(a) The deaths were distributed as follows:

British Isles (army only)	704,803
Canada	56,639
Australia	59,330
New Zealand	16,302
South Africa	6,606
Newfoundland	1,204
India	62,056
Colonies	49,763

(b) On the Western Front 560,000 were killed or died of
disease: in the Gallipoli campaign 26,213.

France

French casualties were slightly higher than the British, the
dead exceeding one million.

Russia

No reliable figures have ever been given. An estimate of 1,700,000 dead has been made, but this is probably an under-estimate.

Italy

An estimate of 460,000 dead is believed to be reliable.

Germany

The official total for killed was given as just over two million; but this figure is disputed by most authorities. The 'Lists of Honour', published by regiments and giving names, amounted to a total of approximately four million.

Austria

The total was given as 7,481,600 killed, wounded and prisoners—of whom 1,728,483 were prisoners.

Turkey

The number of dead was estimated at 300,000.

It is impossible to calculate with accuracy the death roll for the whole war, combatants and civilians, in all countries. A figure of 30 million has been given, and it is probably a considerable under-estimate. In addition many millions were maimed, or made invalids for life, and vast numbers lost their homes and their possessions.

When Germany invaded Belgium on 4th August 1914, she initiated a sequence of events which has no parallel in history. It did not end with the Armistice of 1918: the consequences are still with us today.

8

COMMENTS ON MILITARY OPERATIONS ON THE WESTERN FRONT

July to November 1918

The preceding chapters describing the fighting on the Western Front are mostly factual. Too much comment would have disturbed the sequence of the story, and such comment as there is has been confined to matters necessary for a proper understanding of events. This chapter is intended to correct this omission by discussing, in general terms, some of the more important features of the last phase of the campaign.

FOCH'S STRATEGIC DESIGN

There seems to be little doubt that by about mid-June 1918, if not earlier, Marshal Foch had formed the opinion that a strategy aimed at breaking *through* the German defences in France and Belgium was very unlikely to succeed. At that time the Supreme Commander had concluded that the German offensive of the spring and early summer had nearly shot its bolt, and his mind was pondering the methods to be used when the Allies resumed the offensive.

War on the continent of Europe had been Foch's life study, and he had behind him four years' experience in operations on the Western Front. Since trench warfare had begun during the winter of 1914–15 he had seen many offensives—Loos, the Somme and Passchendaele by the Allies; Verdun, the recent

offensives of March and April 1918 and others by the Germans.
In every case it had been comparatively easy to break *in* to the
defenders' position, but the attempt to exploit the initial success
with a break *through*, with decisive results, had always failed.
In most cases the only gain was a few square miles of devastated
country, at a cost of tens of thousands of casualties with little
more, or even less, loss to the enemy. In other cases the pause
following the initial attack allowed the defender to carry out a
planned withdrawal to a previously prepared defensive position
and, by this means, maintain an unbroken front.

The Marshal no doubt asked himself if, in these coming
battles which he was planning, there were any new conditions,
or any new method available, which would enable a break *in*
to be followed by a break *through*, and operations which would
turn a successful attack into a decisive victory. Faced with
highly organized German defences in depth, the Allied horsed
cavalry was too vulnerable, and its radius of action too limited,
to exploit success to a break *through* stage. Allied tanks were too
few in numbers, too slow and too unreliable mechanically for
the purpose. Moreover, they were not organized for an independent mobile rôle. Foch was caught by a hiatus in the mobile
arm: horsed cavalry had become obsolete and the *blitzkrieg*
tank had not yet been developed.

In these circumstances Foch came to the conclusion that the
old strategy of piling up vast numbers of men, and vast material
resources, for a sustained offensive aiming at a break *through*
was doomed to failure. This was confirmed by General
Weygand after the war when approached on the matter by
Brigadier-General Sir James Edmonds, who was responsible for
compiling the British official histories of World War I. Weygand
stated emphatically that when planning the coming offensive
Foch never contemplated a break *through* or even a deep
penetration.

Foch's method was to attack in much the same manner as
before; but with only a short preliminary bombardment in
order to secure surprise. His plan was to discontinue the attack
as soon as enemy resistance hardened. The frontage of the attack
would then be extended on either flank or a new offensive,

or offensives, be staged on another sector of the front. That this method was the correct one was proved by events: to Marshal Foch must go the credit of introducing this new form of strategy on the Western Front. He believed that by this means the Germans would become so weakened, and their reserves so dissipated, that they would no longer be able to hold the front. It may be he thought that in the very final stage a break-through might be achieved and the disintegration of the German Army brought about. But this did not happen: the German front remained unbroken until the day of the Armistice. Many people believe that the enemy was on the point of military collapse, but this is questionable.

ALLIED RESERVES

It is a military maxim, and one which appears with regularity in military textbooks, that the commander of a force must always retain a reserve in his own hand. Indeed, once the battle has started the employment of his reserve is the main means by which he can influence its outcome. When he has expended his reserve he must set about the task of forming a new one. It is therefore surprising to find that at no time during his period as Supreme Commander did Foch have a reserve at his personal disposal. At one time, in January 1918, three months before Foch became Supreme Commander, it was proposed that a reserve be formed for the Versailles Supreme War Council. It was to consist of British, French and Italian divisions; but all the Commanders-in-Chief protested and the proposal was dropped.

It is of course true that both Haig and Pétain, and later Pershing, had their own reserves which in theory could be switched by Foch from one Allied front to another in an emergency. Similarly each of Haig's and Pétain's army commanders, and in many cases Corps commanders, had their reserve divisions. But these 'national' reserve divisions varied in number from time to time, and were very often earmarked for specific tasks. Not infrequently they were divisions which had been badly mauled in battle and would not become fully

battleworthy until rested and made up to strength. Foch could
never rely with certainty on these divisions to meet an emergency or take advantage of a fleeting opportunity. During the
early phase of the German spring offensive in March and April,
when the main onslaught was against the British front, Pétain
was more than tardy in providing French divisions to support
Haig. Always when Foch wanted to use part of the reserve of one
of his Commanders-in-Chief there were hesitance and excuses;
acquiescence was often with an ill grace.

RELATIONS BETWEEN HAIG, PÉTAIN AND PERSHING

Although Marshal Foch was styled Supreme Commander of the
Allied Land Forces he was never in absolute control. Even his
directive from the Allied governments made that clear (*see*
Chapter 1). He was responsible for strategic direction, but was
to leave the tactical conduct of the battle to the Commanders-
in-Chief of the three major national forces. Being a French
general, fighting on French soil, he naturally had more control
over Pétain than he had over Haig and Pershing. When on 15th
July 1918 Pétain cancelled a previously arranged offensive,
because the Germans had attacked in force elsewhere, Foch
promptly countermanded the order and the offensive proceeded
as planned (*see* Chapter 3). This was something he could not
have done in so brusque a manner with Haig. There would have
been consultation and persuasion rather than an order. Foch
had no power to dismiss or appoint a British or American
general and could not have done so in the French Army
without poaching on Pétain's prerogative. He had no say in
training, organization, administration or discipline.

In spite of the high-sounding title of his appointment it is
clear that Foch had little control except in the field of strategic
direction, and even in that field he could not always rely on
unhesitating compliance. In July 1918, when Foch requested
Haig to prepare an offensive in the Béthune area, Haig
objected and proposed instead an operation on the Amiens
front in conjunction with the French First Army (*see* Chapter 2).
This was clearly a decision under the heading of 'strategic

direction'; but nevertheless Haig's view prevailed and the Amiens offensive took place—with very satisfactory results. This is only one of a number of differences of opinion between Foch and Haig.

There was also some friction with Pershing, particularly over the latter's persistence that American troops should be concentrated under American leadership and fight as a national army rather than dispersed under French and British commanders. During the crisis period of the German offensives in March and April Pershing placed those units of his troops which were properly equipped and battleworthy at Foch's disposal for use as and where the situation demanded *—a fine gesture in the common interest. But as soon as the crisis had passed Pershing, backed by his own government, insisted on pushing on with his plans for American troops to fight as a national army.

Foch and his three Commanders-in-Chief all had their difficulties. Foch had immense responsibilities without the ability to order—only to persuade and suggest. Haig had the difficult task of serving under the direction of a Supreme Commander with whose views he did not always agree, at a time when he did not have the full confidence of his own Prime Minister. Sir James Edmonds, who served on Haig's staff in the war, was in the habit of describing Haig's opponents as threefold, 'Boche, Foch and Lloyd George'—a slight exaggeration perhaps, but a statement with a grain of truth. Pershing had all the disadvantages of a 'new boy', but one with immense potential power should the war continue into 1919. Pétain, in dealing with a fellow Frenchman as his superior, probably had the easiest rôle.

Alliances in war are notoriously difficult to keep free from friction. The Anglo-American alliance, in World War II, with its integrated military staffs, did not always work perfectly, and

*Although at the end of March 1918 there were about 319,000 American troops in France, many were administrative personnel and the fighting arms were deficient in artillery and other heavy equipment. At the crisis period of March and April the Americans could only be used as part of British and French formations. They were not yet in a condition to fight as a separate army.

the overall commanders in the field—whether American or British—had considerably more power than Foch ever possessed in 1918.

All in all, the system of command on the Western Front, between March and November 1918, worked as well as could reasonably be expected. There was never a disagreement amounting to a crisis. Throughout a very difficult period Foch and his three subordinates showed a high degree of responsibility, common sense and tact. The Alliance was well served by these four men. Together they won the war several months earlier than most people had expected.

It would seem that Haig was the first to realize that victory was possible in 1918. Better than anyone else he appreciated the loss of morale and fighting qualities in the German Army, evinced by the highly successful British attack of 8th August. From then onwards his efforts were devoted to winning the war before the severe winter weather began and he seems to have imbued his subordinates with the same spirit.

It is evident that when the Allied offensives began at the end of July (during the Second Battle of the Marne) Foch had no thoughts of an early victory. His instructions aimed at limited objectives, with a view to creating favourable conditions for more ambitious operations later. Initially he wanted to improve the French and Belgian economies by freeing some of the coal-mining and industrial areas, and certain important strategic railways. He gave no indication that the end was in sight: that did not come until much later. It is of course possible that he did not wish to be over-optimistic and create the impression—particularly among his volatile fellow countrymen—that a slackening of effort was now permissible or that there was no need to prepare for another winter, spring and summer of war.

In all fairness I think that the credit must be given to Haig for being the first man in authority to realize that the war could be won in 1918, and it was the troops under his command who played the major part in bringing this about.

COMMENT ON BRITISH AND ALLIED TACTICS
IN THE FINAL STAGES

The comments which follow are based on the experiences of British troops, but in general they apply equally to those of other nationalities serving on the Western Front.

The soldiers who fought in France and Belgium in the last stages of the war had previously experienced only static warfare or, if they had come out as reinforcements, had been trained mostly in the requirements of trench warfare. In this type of fighting little tactical skill was necessary. Ability to march under a heavy load, use a few simple weapons and dig, and the possession of a stout heart and a good constitution—these were the main requirements. For junior leaders and the men under them life had become a routine. Even in the attack the troops conformed to a standard drill.

Although senior officers realized that before the fighting ended there was likely to be a spell of open warfare, and some lip service was given to training for it, in practice very little was done. Among junior officers it was regarded as something very remote: they had quite enough to do keeping their men fit and up to the mark for trench warfare. Consequently, when the Allied offensives began in earnest in August, the troops were unprepared for the more fluid operations which followed, still less prepared for the semi-open warfare of September and early October and somewhat mystified by the degree of manœuvre and flexibility required during the final four or five weeks.

It is of considerable interest to follow the manner in which this change from trench warfare to open warfare took place, and the way the troops fought. The junior leader of 1915–17 had many trials, tribulations and dangers to contend with, but he was not expected to show much initiative. In a defensive battle his duty was to persuade his men to hold the position or die in the attempt. In attack his section, platoon or company moved forward, in a previously rehearsed drill formation, on to a close and usually well-defined objective. Those who were lucky enough to arrive there dug in and prepared to repel the inevitable counter-attack. There was rarely any question of pushing on, or a junior leader exploiting a favourable situation. If he did so he would probably run into his own side's artillery fire, which had been carefully planned to a timed programme. The only opportunity for an infantry junior leader to show initiative was on patrol, at which many had become highly skilled, both by day and by night.

The main characteristic of the fighting from August 1918 onwards was the increasing distance which Allied troops could, and were expected to, advance in an attack. This was to some extent due to the weakening resistance of the enemy, but mainly to the fact that he was carrying out a series of planned withdrawals. In the latter case the initial attacks were frequently against weak rearguards—usually consisting of machine-gun teams supported by artillery. Having delayed the attackers, and often inflicted heavy casualties, these rearguards withdrew, perhaps two or three or even more miles. This enabled the attackers to continue the advance; but, unless there was to be a long halt, and a waste of time which could not be afforded in the shortening hours of daylight, further progress had to be made on the initiative of junior leaders—company, platoon and section commanders. This was a kind of warfare for which they had not been trained.

As the Allied offensive progressed, so the operations became more and more fluid. The German defences became thinner on the ground and their bounds back from one position to the next longer. An increasing responsibility rested on junior leaders to push on without waiting for orders from above.

In the very last phase, in November, operations on some parts of the front assumed the character of open warfare as visualized in the 1914 textbooks, and of the kind practised in Europe in the early weeks of war, and in some overseas theatres such as Palestine and Mesopotamia. Mobile columns were formed, covered by cavalry detachments followed by an advanced guard of infantry, artillery, perhaps a few tanks and a strong detachment of engineers to deal with demolitions, road craters and booby-traps. It was the duty of these columns to overcome minor opposition and push on again as quickly as possible. If strong resistance was encountered the troops of the column were expected to report enemy dispositions and strength back to the main column so that arrangements could be made for a co-ordinated attack to deal with the situation. For the troops of the mobile columns this often entailed deploying and returning to march formation two or three times in a single day. It is not surprising that troops who had not practised the close co-operation between arms which this kind of warfare demanded made many mistakes, were at times hesitant and generally manœuvred in a clumsy manner. The conditions were very different from the trench warfare to which they were accustomed.

From the point of view of minor tactics the Germans enjoyed many advantages in these last weeks. Machine-guns and artillery were the ideal weapons for rearguard actions of this kind. Being in retreat they were able to reconnoitre their positions, range their artillery and arrange their communications in comparative leisure. These were advantages not enjoyed by the advancing troops. Moreover, in operations of this kind one or two well-sited machine-guns have very great delaying power, and the German machine-gunners were picked men and very gallant fighters. Offensive operations, particularly in the last week of the war, were hampered by very wet weather.

As a result of these conditions the progress made by the Allies was often slow, even when opposition was slight or non-existent. An advance of four or five miles a day was good, eight or ten very good. The popular conception of a victorious army sweeping forward with horses at the gallop and men at the double was not to be seen on the Western Front in the autumn of 1918.

It is not unreasonable to ask why the troops had not been trained to meet the conditions of open warfare which were almost certain to come about in the final stages of the war. That is a valid question, but it is not one which is likely to be asked by anyone who has held a responsible position in a major theatre of war in which fighting goes on continuously day after day. In these circumstances training is always difficult, especially the higher form of training involving the co-operation of all arms on a major scale. It was almost impossible in a country such as France during the First World War, where every acre of available land was devoted to agriculture. In addition British troops had not fully recovered from the losses of the retreats of the spring and early summer. Many units had suffered heavy casualties and had either not had their losses made good, or contained a high proportion of newly joined officers and men in their ranks.

Between mid-August and mid-November 1918 the British Army on the Western Front carried out a remarkable series of offensive operations in very unfavourable conditions. Through no fault of their own the troops were untrained for the kind of operations involved: they were carried forward to victory more by high morale and good discipline than by tactical skill.

ADMINISTRATION

As explained earlier administration had been comparatively simple in trench warfare. Rations, ammunition and other commodities were delivered to a more or less routine programme. The troops were well fed and the sick and wounded promptly and well cared for. This procedure was not very greatly disturbed by the limited offensive operations of 1915–17.

When, however, the troops began to move forward at a greater pace in the advance to victory, different and sometimes unforeseen problems arose. The troops were more scattered than previously. A commanding officer could never say in the early morning where his headquarters or his sub-units would be at dusk. It was not uncommon for an infantry battalion commander to end the day's fighting and be unaware of the exact location of all his companies. It must be remembered that, except at higher formation headquarters, there were no field wireless sets or motor-cycle dispatch riders. Telephone lines took time to lay and were easily cut: very often the only means of communication was a man on his feet.

Recent interviews with a number of people of varying ranks and arms of the service who took part in these operations confirm that there was little difficulty in lifting the daily requirements in rations, ammunition, etc. The difficulty was to locate headquarters and units and ensure that supplies were delivered at the right place at the right time. The almost unanimous view, however, was that throughout the period the troops were well fed, and that the wounded and sick were evacuated promptly and were well cared for.

Difficulties were, however, experienced in delivering some of the more unusual types of heavy equipment, such as bridging material, material for repairing roads, assault boats and other commodities and equipment requiring heavy-wheeled transport for its conveyance. The bad condition of the roads, the wet weather and enemy demolitions often made this a slow process.

Had the operations gone on longer, and the front moved farther east, the troops would have got farther from their established railheads. This, at a time when motor transport was limited, would have created very real problems. These are discussed in the next chapter.

MORALE AND DISCIPLINE

Throughout history great commanders have emphasized the importance of morale in war. Napoleon rated the relative importance of moral qualities compared to material matters as three to one, and Field-Marshal Lord Montgomery records that there can be no success without high morale. Closely allied to morale is discipline. A man may have good morale, but still be ill-disciplined by being badly behaved, unpunctual and disobedient. The good soldier is well-disciplined as well as having high morale.

The dual quality of morale/discipline is hard to define. The British soldier, even when his morale is good, is inclined to grouse. Very often his morale is highest when the situation is at its worst, as at Mons and the First Battle of Ypres in 1914 and at Dunkirk in 1940. He thrives on action and periodical crises. When things are quiet he becomes bored and his morale has to be sustained by competitive games, adventure and other artificial means; his discipline by insistence on smartness, instant obedience to orders and strict punctuality.

As a result of experience in command of fighting troops in

two World Wars I think that the most important factor in maintaining morale and discipline is that the soldier should have confidence in his leaders. He does not expect his officers to be particularly clever; but he does expect them to devote their whole energies to his well-being, to have a sense of humour, to appear fearless in action and, above all, to be strictly impartial and fair. It will not be out of place to quote a few examples of the measures taken to promote good morale which are within my own knowledge.

The daily duty, which in civil life is normally performed after breakfast in the smallest room in the house, is often difficult to fit in during active operations. Yet it is essential to good health. In the good unit this is realized and the necessary time provided at suitable intervals. Similarly, even in very bad winter conditions in the trenches, the good officer made special arrangements for his men to wash and shave daily.

The censorship of outgoing mail and the prompt delivery of incoming letters were matters that could easily be overlooked in times of crisis. In a good unit it was a point of honour to see that mail was handled promptly, even in the heat of battle.

During periods of rest hot baths and facilities for washing clothing were often difficult to come by; but the resourceful officer was always able to improvise some means.

The personal problems of his men were part of a junior officer's duties—domestic troubles at home, the desire to be with a friend in another platoon or company, even money matters and problems of religion: all these, and many others, came the way of the regimental officer who had his men's confidence.

These may appear to be trivial matters, but strict attention to details of this kind represented the difference between good and bad morale.

On the Western Front in World War I, except at the very beginning and very end, there was little scope for tactical skill. In the field of military technique the requirements were simple. By 1916 officers who had started the war as subalterns had little difficulty in commanding infantry battalions as lieutenant-colonels. By 1917 and 1918 some officers who had joined after the outbreak of war held that rank and commanded perhaps a thousand men in battle. For these men there was one indispensable qualification: they had to be good man-managers; it was essential that the regimental officer should be able to maintain a high standard of morale and discipline. That was the secret of success and the hall-mark of the good officer. That the British Army as a whole was successful in this respect—not only in 1914–18, but again in 1939–45—is shown by the fact that the British Empire was the only belligerent to take part in both contests from beginning to end without experiencing a serious mutiny or mass acts of ill-discipline in the armed forces.

In August 1918, after fighting a series of gruelling defensive battles since the previous March, losing much ground and epuipment and many men, the British Army turned round and within three months had played the major rôle in dealing the enemy a mortal blow. This was a very remarkable feat of arms which has never been given the credit and publicity which it deserved. It could only have been done by an army whose morale and discipline were soundly based, and that it was so done was due to its leadership—from the Commander-in-Chief down to the humblest corporal commanding a section. A German officer is on record as saying that the British Army of 1914–18 consisted of 'lions commanded by donkeys', and a British writer thought fit to write a book on that theme. But that does not happen; those with experience prefer Napoleon's well-known maxim, 'There are no bad men, only bad officers.'

It is perhaps not inappropriate to end this dissertation on morale by giving two quotations which, more than two decades later, appeared regularly on the headquarter notice-boards, and at the top of all correspondence of two units—the first an Engineer unit in Burma; the second an Armoured unit in the Western Desert.

> We do the impossible immediately: miracles take a little longer.

> We can do it. What is it?

The cynical may dub these as childish; but they typify the spirit which wins campaigns and battles.

9

IN RETROSPECT

Too often comment in retrospect consists of being clever after the event—in other words saying what should, or should not, have been done, but failing to make proper allowance for the advantages of after-knowledge. This kind of comment in retrospect is valueless, often misleading and invariably unfair to individuals. If, however, we examine past events in a sensible manner we can bring the full benefit of experience to bear on solving present and future problems. We must remember that the men who had to make decisions often possessed only a fraction of the information available to their critics and often had only a matter of hours, or even minutes, to decide very weighty matters. The critic on the other hand sits at ease at his desk, surrounded by books of reference and with almost limitless opportunities and sources for filling in the gaps in his knowledge.

In war the difference in opportunity between the leader and his critics is even greater than in peaceful fields of activity. The former's decisions are often split-second decisions and he is opposed by an enemy doing all he can to disguise his intentions and frustrate his opponent. The post-war critic on the other hand usually has the plans and dispositions of both sides at his disposal.

This book is mainly concerned with the period of the

Armistice; but in considering events in retrospect it will be useful to consider the 1914–18 War as a whole in general terms, before particularizing on the period on the Western Front covered by the previous chapters—July to November 1918.

THE WAR IN GENERAL, AUGUST 1914–NOVEMBER 1918

SURPRISES AND CHANGES

World War I was a war of surprises and changes. There were three main surprises:

First, the duration of the war. Politicians, financiers and service chiefs alike expected it to last a matter of weeks or at the most months. Only Lord Kitchener forecast, from the very start, a long war; but even he did not think it would last as long as four years and three months.

Second, the intensity of the struggle. It had never been contemplated that the great civilized Christian nations of the world would slaughter millions of their young men in order to produce results which, as far as we can see, have in the long run been harmful to all.

Third, in the actual land fighting it had not been realized how greatly the defence would predominate over the offence. All the armies of the great powers had been trained for offensive action, and this led to very heavy casualties—particularly in the French Army—in the early days of the war. By the beginning of the first winter (end of October 1914) the vast forces facing each other on the Western Front had shot their bolt as far as offensive action was concerned, and had begun to construct the elaborate systems of defence which were to last for four years of trench warfare. In other theatres of operations —where the forces engaged were smaller and there were open flanks—trench warfare was less in evidence, although in nearly every theatre it was adopted somewhere, at some time; but never to the same extent as on the Western Front. There, as has been explained in earlier chapters, the defences of both sides defied all attempts to break through. The manpower of

Europe, supported by guns, tanks and other devices, could dent, but could not break through, the systems of earthworks manned by resolute men equipped with modern weapons and protected by barbed wire. In vain the massed cavalry of both sides waited, poised to exploit the break-through which never came.

Never before had war been waged on such a worldwide scale, by so many combatants, for so long. Instead of two combat elements, land and sea, a new one, the air, was coming into use. These factors, combined with the remarkable progress in engineering and science, were the beginning of a transition in warfare. It cannot be said that the changes were revolutionary; they were merely the start of trends which were to reach fruition a quarter of a century later. World War I ended with the horsed cavalryman still regarded as the main arm for reconnaissance and pursuit—with always the chance of a charge in the grand manner. As yet the tank was too slow, too cumbersome and too unreliable to replace the horseman in this rôle.* The aeroplane played a useful, but not a decisive, rôle. It was used mainly for reconnaissance and, as a fighter, to drive off enemy reconnaissance aircraft. With the formation of the Royal Air Force on 1st April 1918, encouragement was given to independent air action, and by the end of the war a British independent bomber force was in existence. But its range of action and bomb load were too limited to make its activities much more than of nuisance value. As early as 1915 German airships ('Zeppelins') had bombed London and parts of south-east England; but here again they were no more than an irritation and soon became vulnerable to attack by aeroplanes firing tracer (luminous) ammunition and anti-aircraft fire.

In this war mechanical transport was employed for the first time and on a very large scale. But its use was confined to back areas and administrative duties. Practically all tactical vehicles —guns, machine-gun and ammunition limbers and other transport of fighting units—was horse- or mule-drawn. The only

* As late as 1923 Lord Haig gave it as his opinion that horsed cavalry would always play a part in war.

exceptions were tanks (used from September 1916 onwards to support infantry in the attack) and an occasional motor ambulance. For long moves infantry were sometimes carried in motor transport (usually civilian double-deck buses painted grey), but 'debussing' usually took place some miles behind the firing line.

In land warfare the change in fighting units—apart from the advent of tanks—was slight. Weapons changed in detail, but remained basically the same. Senior officers rode horses, and horses and mules pulled vehicles of much the same pattern in 1918 as in 1914. In base areas and on the lines of communication the motor vehicle had largely, but not entirely, replaced the horse-drawn vehicle.

At sea the only major change during the war was the increasing importance of the submarine which, in the case of German submarines, operated against merchant shipping as well as against warships.

In 1914 the military aircraft of all the belligerents were numbered in hundreds. By 1918 there were many thousands.

Although the changes on record are perhaps less than might have been expected in a war of over four years' duration between highly industrialized nations, it is interesting to recollect that, as far as land warfare was concerned, the tide was about to turn. Had hostilities lasted into 1919 Britain would have produced and operated a large mechanical army of many thousands of tanks and their supporting vehicles (*see* Chapter 2).

MILITARY AND POLITICAL LEADERSHIP

Of the six major powers—Britain, France, Russia, Italy, Germany and Austria-Hungary—all but Britain began the war with large conscript armies. Their cadres of regular officers and trained junior leaders were tailored to meet the requirements of forces numbered in millions. It was very different with Britain, who had a regular army of only some 250,000, of whom about half were serving overseas. Britain began the war with a tiny army of high-class professionals (the original British Expeditionary Force comprised only 6 divisions and 5 cavalry brigades against France's 72 infantry and cavalry divisions and Germany's 98). She ended it with a large amateur army led by a few professionals.

Until the army reforms, initiated by Lord Haldane and brought into operation in 1908, Britain had not contemplated participation in a war on the continent of Europe, and even after 1908 had never envisaged a war lasting anything like as long as four years, nor a British Army of some 60 divisions playing the major rôle in the final assault on Imperial Germany —and in addition defeating Turkey almost single-handed and also providing forces to fight Austria-Hungary and Bulgaria.

There had been no big war in Europe since the Franco-Prussian War of 1870-1. The Russian Army had some salutary experiences in the Russo-Japanese War of 1904-5; but apart from that the General Staffs of Europe had no war experience. They had, however, fairly clear-cut military problems, the most obvious being a war with France and Russia against Germany and Austria-Hungary. These problems had been studied in the minutest detail at continental war ministries, staff colleges and at war games. When the flag fell in August 1914 the rival continental armies were as ready for war as the somewhat cumbersome methods of mobilization and deployment permitted. They had built up their armies in peace: Britain had to build up hers after the declaration of war.

On 6th August—two days after Britain declared war—Field-Marshal Lord Kitchener became Secretary of State for War. He very soon convinced his Cabinet colleagues that the war was likely to be a long one, and that the government and country must face up to the task of raising an army of continental size. In the early days the new armies (known as 'Kitchener's Armies') had little more than an abundance of enthusiasm. There was an acute shortage of equipment, even uniforms and rifles, and training was hampered by the inexperience of the officers. The first of the Kitchener's Army divisions took the field in the late summer of 1915, when four divisions took part in the Battle of Loos in September. In the twelve months' hiatus, between the outbreak of war and the entry into the contest of divisions of newly raised troops, Britain had to scrape the bottom of the barrel in order to maintain, and expand as far as possible, her armies in the field. The B.E.F. in France was very considerably increased by the addition of two divisions from home originally earmarked for home defence, other troops gathered from overseas stations and replaced by territorials and by two Indian divisions—the last not an ideal choice for static warfare in Europe during the exceptionally severe winter of 1914–15. Many individual territorial units were also sent to France in 1914 and early 1915.

This, in the briefest terms, is the background to the main problem confronting Britain in the early months of the war— the raising, in double quick time, of a large modern army to fight Germans who had been trained to arms on a national scale for generations. It is not surprising that difficulties arose and mistakes were made. The 'dilution' in the army was very great. Regular officers who began the war as subalterns and captains were lieutenant-colonels by Christmas 1914 and generals by 1916 and 1917. Retired officers (known as 'dug-outs') found themselves assuming responsibilities beyond their wildest expectations when they retired—by inclination or because they could not pass their promotion examinations! Men who were lance-corporals in 1914 found themselves as sergeants and sergeant-majors—in many cases officers—by 1915 and 1916. Many of the old army were not, of course, available for these promotions: a high proportion of the regimental officers and men were killed or permanently incapacitated at Mons, Le Câteau, First Ypres and during the winter war of 1914–15.

In the higher ranks the responsibilities increased in propor- tion. Haig, who at the beginning of the campaign in France commanded a Corps of some 40,000 men, was Commander-in- Chief by the summer of 1916 with around two million men under him.

Since 1918 the higher command of all the belligerents have come under heavy fire, sometimes from those who served under them, but mainly from historians and journalists who specialize in military affairs. This criticism has been accentuated since 1945, partly because World War II revived interest in military matters, and partly because the critics were able to compare the generalship of 1914–18 unfavourably with the more spectacular accomplishments of the generals of 1939–45. In particular Haig has been singled out for criticism by the armchair critics. It is obviously not possible in a book of this kind to discuss the higher direction of the war in detail, but a few remarks of a general nature, centred round Haig, will not be out of place.

The main criticism of all the commanders in Europe has been that they squandered men in large numbers in unsuccessful attempts to break through their opponents' front. In recent years Haig has been vilified as the arch-protagonist of frontal attacks at immense loss of life. In this respect he has been compared unfavourably with the generals of World War II who fought their battles more economically and, so it is alleged, in a more professional manner than by engaging in head-on frontal attacks. In considering this matter two factors must be borne in mind:

1. The very obvious one that Haig had no enemy flanks to attack and no alternative to frontal attacks.
2. That by World War II the pendulum had swung in favour of the offensive over the defensive. This had been brought about mainly by the fast-moving tank which subdued fire, crushed obstacles, killed many of the enemy and pursued the survivors; and by tactical aircraft which played havoc with rear areas, by bombing enemy guns, reserve troops and transport.

It is interesting to note that in two operations in which Lord Montgomery had no flanks and was forced to attack frontally— El Alamein and the attacks around Caen in the Normandy beach-head—he also experienced great difficulties. At El Alamein he took twelve days to secure a break-through: the battle was a very close-run thing against an opponent fighting at a considerable disadvantage in numbers, and with grave shortages of petrol and ammunition. At Caen the circumstances were similar and the very marked Allied air superiority put a big check on German reinforcements and supplies. In these two operations Montgomery had two weapons at his disposal which Haig never had—a powerful tactical air force and a large force of long-range, fast-moving tanks capable of turning a break-in into a break-through. Without these it is questionable if Montgomery's frontal attacks would have been any more successful than Haig's. As it was, the break-out from the Normandy beach-head took place far to the west on the American front; although this climax was, of course, greatly helped by the British hammer-blows in the Caen area; that was the essence of the strategic plan.

In considering Haig there are two points on which he has been heavily criticized, namely that he persisted in his attacks for too long—after the enemy had been alerted and the chances of success were small—and that the principle of always counter-attacking to recover every inch of ground lost in a local enemy attack was costly in lives and bad for morale. These are reasonable criticisms which merit investigation.

Haig's persistence in continuing attacks and thereby incurring heavy losses was due to his search for a break-through which, in many of his offensive operations, must have seemed to him to be just round the corner. This was faulty judgement; but it was a fault which he shared with every other national commander on the Western and Italian fronts up to the summer of 1918. The alternative was the method adopted by Foch of dealing a series of surprise hammer-blows, each being halted when it had shot its bolt. By this means it was hoped that the enemy would use up his reserves, be unable to hold the front and his army would disintegrate. This never quite happened, but maybe it was approaching that point by the day of the Armistice. This method certainly brought the Germans to the point of asking for an Armistice and accepting conditions which were not far short of unconditional surrender. To Marshal Foch must go the credit of evolving and carrying out this plan. It is, however, only fair to record that as overall commander he was the only man capable of carrying out a strategy which required a co-ordinated series of attacks along the whole Allied front. Neither Haig nor Pétain could do this; and they do not seem to have advocated such a strategy at any time.

The second point—the question of local counter-attacks—is

one on which opinion at the time was sharply divided at all
levels of command. Those against said that the loss of a few
square yards, or acres, of ground was in itself of no consequence,
and only became so if some important tactical feature had been
lost, or if there was no tenable alternative position to link up
with the defences on the flanks. If this was not so, as was very
often the case, it was contended that the heavy losses, which
were very often sustained in these counter-attacks, were not
justified and had a very bad effect on morale. This view was not
accepted by many people, among them a high proportion of
junior ranks, who had most to lose even in a successful counter-
attack. They maintained that the realization among the
defenders that, if a position was lost it would have to be
recaptured by them or troops from their own or a neighbouring
unit, induced a determination and resolution in the defence
which would not otherwise have existed. They further maintained that a general acceptance that loss of ground did not
matter much would result in slackness, and a decline in the will
to hold on, which could have very serious results. Moreover, as
the war progressed, and the trench systems became more
elaborate, the loss of only a small sector could mean the loss of
valuable dug-out shelter and protection and, very important
indeed, the dislocation of mining operations, which had
become a feature of trench warfare by 1916, and the loss of
mining personnel. I think there is no doubt that at the time the
balance of opinion among front line officers was in favour of
counter-attacks of this kind: it was certainly so in my own unit *
in 1915–16.

The matter can be summarized like this. In defence it has
always been a principle in the British Army that a position is
held 'to the last man and the last round', which implies that
every defensive position, or sector, is vital to the defence as a
whole. This being so a position overrun by the enemy must be
recaptured. If it had become the custom not to attempt to
recapture a lost position the validity of the 'last man and last

---

* The 1st Battalion The Cameronians (Scottish Rifles), who went to France
with the original B.E.F. in 1914. By the winter of 1915–16 the battalion had
only 3 pre-war officers and about 70 pre-war other ranks serving with it.

round' principle would have been in doubt. This could have had very grave results. Looking back it may be thought that this was a minor tactical matter of little importance. At the time it was not regarded in that light: it was a constant topic of conversation among junior officers. The observance of the principle cost a lot of lives, and it was a matter affecting morale and discipline which it is difficult for anyone to appreciate who has not participated in defensive warfare under 1915–18 conditions for a considerable period. It was also a matter which involved the higher command in considerable criticism both during and after the war—mostly from armchair critics. The local counter-attack, as practised by the British on the Western Front, when examined closely by experienced people, was not so foolhardy as it seemed, or resented by those most closely concerned—the regimental officers and men who had to carry out these attacks.

Similar criticism has sometimes been raised in connection with the many raids which were a feature of British tactics in trench warfare. These raids varied in scale from small platoon operations to large raids at battalion strength. Sometimes they were for intelligence purposes to obtain identifications: more often they were for purely tactical reasons. Well planned and skilfully carried out they achieved a high proportion of successes, and were undoubtedly valuable in maintaining morale and the fighting spirit of the troops.

In considering the criticism of Haig—and indeed all the generals of this war—that they squandered lives recklessly, one must not overlook the circumstances in which they fought, so very different from those twenty-five years later. They operated in an era when human ingenuity in the defence was greater than it was in attack. Until the arrival of the tank there was no answer to the hidden and concrete-protected machine-gun. With new weapons, the experience and the usually open flanks of 1939–45, the generals of World War II had better chances of showing their skill than their 1914–18 predecessors. It is true to say that the British soldiers of 1914–18 never lost faith in their commanders: with some justification regimental officers were often critical of the staff; but the commanders always had their respect and confidence, and discipline and morale never faltered. It was after the war that criticism of the higher command began, and particularly after World War II when comparison with the generals of 1939–45 made the cult of denigration so much easier.

Operations by the Royal Navy in 1914–18 have been subjected to less criticism than those of the Army. This is due largely to the fact that far fewer served at sea than on land, and also because the Navy's activities were more technical and consequently less understood. We have seen how, as the war progressed, the Army became a body of amateurs led by a few professionals. This was hardly the case with the Navy: although there was some dilution the Senior Service maintained its professional status to a very considerable extent. Moreover, it carried out its war tasks admirably. It protected the country against invasion, allowed us to carry by sea, and deploy, land forces in any part of the world, kept the German surface fleet bottled up in its harbours for most of the war and played a big part in escorting hundreds of thousands of American troops to Europe despite enemy boasts that this could not be done. The only criticism, and that has not been very severe, is that the Navy was slow to get the better of the submarine menace against Allied and neutral shipping. But on the whole the admirals of 1914–18 have had a much better press than the generals.

Consideration of the military leadership leads on to the question of political leadership. This was a matter which had hardly obtruded during the colonial wars of the late nineteenth century, which were fought, and usually won, by the armed forces without any very noticeable efforts on the part of statesmen. In the South African War (1899–1902) political leadership, in the matter of propaganda and defining the aims of the war and general policy for conducting it, was evident; but not to the extent of playing any significant part in the direction of operations or the administration and supply of the services.

In World War I the rôle of the politician was very different. This was a national war in which the whole population was involved: industry to supply the forces with equipment, agriculture to feed the forces and the civil population and various services—such as the merchant service, railways, post office, medical and health, diplomacy and many others—to keep the country going under the strain of a major war.

It was the task of the government to weld all these elements into a national organization to win the war as quickly as possible. It was something in which the politicians were as inexperienced as the other organizations—civil and military—involved.

In his book, *The World Crisis 1911–1918*, Sir Winston Churchill gives it as his opinion that a civilian, by which he implied a politician, is just as capable as an admiral or a general in deciding matters of grand strategy and the broad direction of war. This is an opinion which is not accepted by everyone, although it is generally agreed that the final decision in these higher matters must be made by the politicians. The armed forces are the servants of the government, but the principle must be worked in a sensible manner. Before deciding on military policy the politician must satisfy himself that his designs are militarily possible and desirable. There were several cases in the two world wars where operations of questionable prudence from a military point of view were undertaken for political motives without proper evaluation by both political and military leaders acting together. Gallipoli (1915), the advance on Baghdad (1915), the expedition to Greece (1941) and the German attack on Russia (1941) are a few examples. An interesting case in more recent times worked the other way: the Anglo-French operations against the Suez Canal in 1956 were militarily practicable, and on the point of complete military success, when they had to be suspended for political reasons.

At the beginning of World War I the degree of co-operation between politicians and service leaders, and indeed between the leaders of the two services, left a great deal to be desired. This greatly improved after December 1916 when David Lloyd George became Prime Minister, as it did in France in 1917 when Georges Clemenceau took over the leadership. It is, however, doubtful if any country in World War I attained the

high standard of national co-operation achieved by Britain in
1940–5, or of co-operation between Allies achieved by America
and Britain in 1942–5.

During his war-time premiership Lloyd George displayed
energy and resourcefulness which played a big part in the
Allied victory; but he never completely trusted his service
advisers and was particularly antipathetic towards Haig. He
disliked his methods and doubted his judgement. A Prime
Minister who mistrusts one of his leading subordinates should
dismiss him, but Lloyd George never felt strong enough to
dismiss Haig.

A bitter disagreement arose between those known as
'Easterners' and 'Westerners'. The Easterners believed that as
no decision seemed practicable on the Western Front one should
be sought elsewhere, and with the collapse of Russia in 1917
their argument was strengthened. The Westerners on the
other hand contended that although it might be possible to gain
victories against Bulgars and Turks in remote parts of the
world, this could only be done by weakening the Western
Front, and that defeat on the Western Front would mean
losing the war. Both sides in the dispute had many adherents,
but generally speaking the politicians were Easterners and the
generals Westerners. Naturally Haig was a vehement
Westerner, as was Robertson (Chief of the Imperial General
Staff, 1915–18) and, of course, the French were in favour of
every possible Allied soldier being made available to defend the
unoccupied part of France and evict the enemy from the
occupied area. The Westerners' case was much strengthened
by early failures against the Turks—at Kut-al-Amara in
Mesopotamia and Gallipoli.

The Westerners' view prevailed as, except for comparatively
small forces, those outside Europe were mostly Indian and
other troops from overseas who were in any case more con-
veniently employed in secondary theatres. This is still a matter
of dispute among military analysts, but the fact remains that
our victories against Bulgars and Turks in 1918 contributed
little or nothing to winning the war, which might well have
been lost on the Western Front if Haig had possessed ten or

fifteen divisions less because they had been sent to fight else-where.

It is customary in some service circles to belittle the efforts of politicians, question their motives and generally show a lack of appreciation of their difficulties. Unlike the service leaders, they often have to deal with ill-disciplined subordinates who, even in war, cannot always be *ordered*, but have to be *persuaded*. They belong to a calling where there is no specialized preliminary training as there is in almost all other professions, and in World War I they had no previous experience to guide them. It was the first big war to be waged by democratic govern-ments, apart from the American Civil War. The politicians' tasks were to co-ordinate the war-time activities of everyone—channel the manpower, raw materials, shipping, etc., into the right directions; sustain and direct the fighting services; conduct relations with our Allies and the dominions and colonies of the Empire; arrange the nations' war-time finances and general economy; sustain public morale and direct propaganda against the enemy. In all these activities there was room for friction and, in the circumstances, many mistakes were inevitable. There is no reason to believe that the affairs of the British Empire in 1914–18 were not as well conducted as those of any other of the contending nations; in some cases and in some respects they were obviously conducted much better.

GERMAN SUBMARINE WARFARE: ITS FAILURE AND THE REPERCUSSIONS

A marked feature of both world wars was the political inepti-tude of Germany by bringing against herself forces which made her defeat almost certain. In World War I she provoked America into a declaration of war: in 1941 she attacked Russia, who in the end became her most ruthless enemy and the one responsible for the present division of Germany.

In the early days of the war American policy, led by President Wilson, favoured strict neutrality, although there was a substantial body of Americans who, because of family and racial ties with Britain, would have liked to enter the war at an early stage. After the sinking of the Cunard liner *Lusitania* on 7th May 1915—when 1,198 people, including many Americans, were drowned—the United States Government demanded the cessation of submarine attacks against passenger and neutral ships, and on 1st September 1915 the German Government informed the United States Government that this demand was accepted. During the winter of 1916–17, however, the Germans, following a great struggle between the Kaiser's civilian and military advisers, reverted to unrestricted submarine warfare as being the surest means of winning the war. As a result of this some 2,000 ships were sunk between February and December 1917, of which 1,197 were British. This policy failed in its purpose of starving Britain, although our food stocks were reduced to a dangerously low level. In the event this barbarous method of warfare rebounded on the Germans in the most serious way possible. It was the chief factor in bringing the United States into the war on 6th April 1917.

The failure of U-boat warfare was crucial to Germany and when, by the summer of 1918, it became apparent that the German Navy could not fulfil its promise of preventing the arrival of American troops in Europe, her position became desperate. With the prospect of some 80 American divisions fighting in Europe by the late spring, it was obvious that Germany's position would be worse in 1919 than it was in 1918. This was the main reason why Germany asked for an Armistice and accepted such stiff conditions—and it all stemmed from her mistaken policy of unrestricted submarine warfare.

This aspect of the struggle brings out clearly what was a largely unrecognized principle of war up to 1945—namely that wars can only be won on land. Naval action might contribute to victory and stave off defeat, but alone it never brought victory. Air power was the same. Napoleon's France, the Kaiser's Germany and Hitler's Germany were all subjected to powerful naval action, and the two last to air action as well, but it required victory on land to bring about their final defeat and submission. Nor did novelties, such as poison gas and 'flying bombs', have much more than a nuisance value—until the advent of the nuclear missile in August 1945. Even this new weapon of obliteration is of questionable value, being altogether too destructive for use. We have seen two large-scale wars— Korea (1950–3) and in Vietnam at the time of writing—where nuclear weapons could have been, but have not been, used. In both cases one side possessed overwhelming air strength, but it did not prove decisive. It required land forces, mostly infantry on their feet armed only with their personal weapons, to achieve success—or even a stalemate as in Korea.*

THE AMERICAN BUILD-UP

To show the terrible price Germany paid for her miscalculations of the effect of unrestricted submarine warfare one cannot do better than quote a few figures of the American build-up of forces in France.

The figures for the number of American troops in France, for various months of 1918, are as follows:

March	318,621	(6 complete divisions and 3 incomplete)
April	429,659	
May	651,284	
June	873,691	
July	1,169,062	
August	1,415,128	
November	2,082,137	(34 complete divisions and 8 incomplete).

As previously explained, American divisions were nearly twice the strength in men of British and French divisions. It should, however, be noted that during the six months March to August 1918 no guns, and very little other heavy material, crossed the Atlantic. In these items up to August the Americans were equipped almost entirely from British and French sources. Up to August 1918 621 ships were used to carry American troops to Europe and of these 326 (or just over 52 per cent) were British. On the other hand 95 per cent of the stores for American troops were transported in American vessels.

* At the time of writing the war in Vietnam is still in progress. No decisive success has been obtained by the combined American and South Vietnamese forces, and the duration of hostilities is unpredictable.

THE CHANGE IN THE ALLIED BALANCE OF STRENGTH
ON THE WESTERN FRONT

One of the most striking features of the war on the Western Front was the remarkable change in Allied strengths which took place as the war progressed. This was seen not only in numerical strength but also in the quality of the national armies.

With the first clash of arms in Belgium and France in August 1914, the Allied Order of Battle in terms of divisions was as follows:

	Infantry Divisions	Cavalry Divisions
France	62	10
Britain	4 (2 more on the way)	1
Belgium	6	1

By the beginning of the Somme offensive in July 1916 the figures were as follows:

	Infantry Divisions	Cavalry Divisions
France	about 100	5
Britain	58	3
Belgium	12	1

By the Armistice on 11th November 1918 the approximate figures were:

	Infantry Divisions	Cavalry Divisions
France	100	5
Britain	61	3
Belgium	12	1
America	42 (8 incomplete)	1

A very marked contrast is also to be found in the frontages held by the national armies of the Allies in 1914 and in 1918. During the Battle of the Marne and the advance to the Aisne the British were on a front of about twelve miles; the French on one of some two hundred miles. On the day of the Armistice —on the active part of the front—the British covered a front of

MOLLIENS. 12th August 1918. His Majesty King George V (right), with General Pershing, when he inspected men from every unit in the 33rd American Division which took part in the fighting at Hamel (4th July) and Chipilly (8th August).

PRINCE MAX OF BADEN, Chancellor of the German Empire, October 1918.

ACHIET-LE-PETIT (Battle of Albert), 21st August 1918. A battalion of the 5th British Division advancing to the capture of the village.

PERONNE, 3rd September 1918. Showing a barricade thrown up by the Germans. The photograph was taken soon after the capture of the town by the 5th Australian Division.

some sixty miles, the French about forty miles and the Americans about eighty-five—the American sector being much less active in the final stages.

THE FRENCH ARMY

In the descriptions of the fighting, and in comment, emphasis has been placed on the leading rôle played by British troops, and there can be no doubt—indeed we have it on Marshal Foch's testimony—that in the final weeks of the campaign Douglas Haig's men bore the brunt of the fighting. This is confirmed by German accounts written by eye-witnesses at the time and by historians later.

This may have given a wrong impression of the French Army, which must be corrected. This book deals mainly with the last four months of the war, when Britain had had four years to expand her forces. There had been a time, from August 1914 until well into 1915, when the major share had been borne by the French Army and the British had held only an insignificant length of front, although a very important one where the fighting was usually hottest. For a country of 39,000,000 people (compared with Germany's 65,000,000) the French effort in the early days of the war was a prodigious one.

The French Army suffered two serious setbacks—the first at the very start of the war when their offensive in the south (known as the Battles of the Frontiers) was everywhere repulsed and heavily counter-attacked—the French casualties exceeding 300,000. The effect of these terrible losses was felt throughout the French Army for a long time. The second setback came more than two years later when the French politicians, with British approval, if not support, replaced General Joffre by General Nivelle in December 1916. Nivelle, who had the gift of expressing himself fluently in both French and English, expounded a novel theory of attack and convinced the politicians that he had a recipe for quick victory which had a good chance of success. There may have been some merits in his ideas; but the inept manner in which the plan was carried out destroyed any chances of success. Briefly, his plan was to avoid a continuance of the war of attrition by a massive offensive on a broad front. Instead of operations with limited objectives, he proposed to give the troops distant objectives, the capture of which would cause a deep breach in the enemy front and, so he hoped, the disintegration of his forces. It was postponed more than once, and the security arrangements were highly inefficient. When the attack finally took place in April 1917 the Germans were ready for it. After some early success it eventually failed and the French suffered some 187,000 casualties in a matter of a few days. The serious and widespread French mutinies which took place soon after were a direct result of this abortive offensive.

Neither of these misfortunes was the fault of the French Army of the day. The French offensive in the south in 1914 was part of Plan XVII on which the French based their opening moves in a war with Germany. This reckless form of offensive had been strongly advocated by Colonel Loyzeau de Grandmaison, a French writer on military matters. Although some French generals were fanatically wedded to the principle of attacking in all circumstances, there were others who appreciated the defensive power of modern machine-guns and artillery and had grave doubts. But the optimistic Plan XVII pleased the majority of members of the French General Staff and such political leaders as knew about it, in that if successful it would spare France from invasion and bring the war to an early conclusion.

The appointment of Nivelle, and concurrence in his offensive, was mainly the work of politicians. The generals—British as well as French—were sceptical of the idea from the beginning. It is a tribute to the French Army of World War I that it was able to conduct offensive operations in 1918, following this serious misfortune and its aftermath of lowered morale. This after a campaign of four years in which it had held the front almost alone in the early stages.

INTELLIGENCE

During both world wars it was customary in some quarters to attribute to the Germans almost miraculous powers of espionage and other methods of obtaining their opponents' secrets. German spies were said to be in the highest quarters of the civil service and armed forces, and even in the Government. In 1914 Prince Louis of Battenburg, the First Sea Lord (the present Lord Mountbatten's father) and Lord Haldane were practically branded as traitors by some irresponsible people; yet of all men they were probably the two who did most to prepare our armed forces for a modern war. A network of enemy agents were supposed to carry out their nefarious designs unmolested, reporting our most secret affairs to Berlin by carrier pigeons, and directing the German airships towards London by means of a chain of men flashing electric torches! The chorus of a popular song ended with the words 'God bless old England the home of the Hun'.

On the other hand our own intelligence and security forces were depicted as the merest simpletons, whose amateur efforts permitted our enemies to discover our inner secrets at will and with little difficulty in safeguarding their own.

The true picture was very different. It is now generally accepted that in World War I Allied, particularly British, intelligence and security was far superior to that of our enemies. It will be sufficient to give two examples. Within a few hours of the declaration of war practically every enemy agent in the United Kingdom had been quietly arrested and put under lock and key. It was some time before the enemy even discovered that this had been done: replacements as they arrived were usually quickly arrested, often as they walked down the gangways from their ships. For a substantial period during the war, unknown to the Germans, we were in possession of their naval code and always knew of any fleet movements some time before they took place. These two achievements alone were of inestimable value to the Allied cause.

It is perhaps a valid criticism of British military intelligence

on the Western Front that it was often too optimistic, particularly with regard to enemy morale. In other respects it was
good, and was specially so at forecasting the places and times
of enemy attacks.

A very remarkable piece of security goes to the credit of the
French. In 1917, when large-scale mutinies occurred in the
French Army—54 divisions, or about half the total, being
involved—the Germans never had an inkling of the state of
affairs. If they had they would surely have attacked earlier than
they did in 1918 and put in the main attack of the spring
offensive against the French instead of the British. At that time
a very substantial part of the line was held by French troops of
low morale and discipline. Even at Haig's headquarters they
were unaware of the real extent of these mutinies.

THE LAST PHASE, JULY TO NOVEMBER 1918

Many of the matters which arise in retrospective consideration
of the last phase of the war have been dealt with in earlier parts
of the book—Foch's plan for victory, Haig's realization that
victory was possible in 1918, the ineptness of the troops when
confronted with a sudden change from trench to open warfare
and many other aspects of the advance to victory. There is,
however, one matter which has not been discussed, namely
whether or not the Germans could have continued the struggle
into 1919, and the situation which would have arisen if they
had decided to make the attempt.

Earlier chapters have told how the Germans conducted a
fighting withdrawal in the last weeks, partly to shorten their
line of battle and partly to extend the Allies' lines of communication in front of their railheads in order to increase their
supply difficulties. We have seen that the Allies rarely advanced
more than five or six miles in a day and that to the very end the
German front remained unbroken, defended mainly by artillery
fire and the gallant machine-gunners who formed the rearguards. There had been a number of acts of ill-discipline among
the troops, but these had been mostly in rear areas. The front
line units had remained staunch, although their fighting value

had declined through lack of numbers and exhaustion. Never-theless, right up to the day of the Armistice the German Army on the Western Front remained a formidable fighting force in defence: its offensive power no longer existed.

Although the German leaders, Hindenburg in particular, came to the conclusion early in October that the war must be brought to an end by diplomatic means as soon as possible, this was not entirely due to their lack of faith in the holding capacity of the Western Front. Some may have doubted this capacity; but there were other reasons. Revolution was in the air, not only among the civil population, but in the fleet where the sailors had mutinied and started Soldiers', Sailors' and Workers' Councils on the Bolshevik model. The German leaders had the awful example of Russia, and a representative gathering of front-line officers had given it as their unanimous opinion that the army could not be relied upon to quell an internal revolution. To most of the leaders in Berlin and Spa the important thing was to stop the fighting before extremist elements got the upper hand, and in time to permit of a blood-less transfer to a more democratic, yet responsible, form of government.

This view was fortified by the unquestionably correct opinion of Prince Max, that any terms which Germany would get in 1919 would be harsher than those obtainable in November 1918.

These were the reasons which swayed the majority of German leaders to seek an Armistice at all costs in the autumn of 1918. Hindenburg and many of the other military leaders also had another reason. They had spent their active lives in the German Army, and their whole lives in a military atmosphere. They could not bear the thought of their army surrendering or disintegrating, and returning to the Fatherland as a fugitive rabble or as disarmed prisoners-of-war. Any Armistice terms which would allow the troops to march back under their officers, in formed bodies with their personal arms, received their support, and those conditions were likely only if an early cease-fire could be arranged. As it happened an early Armistice *was* arranged, a violent revolution in Germany was averted and the troops marched home with every appearance of an army which had never been defeated. But what if these counsels had not prevailed and the internal situation had permitted the Germans to go on fighting? It is interesting to speculate how events might have turned out.

Armies of the size of those mustered by the Allies on the Western Front can only be supplied by railways. The railways take supplies forward to within some fifteen to twenty-five miles of the fighting troops, the last stage being done by motor transport and, in 1918, by horse-drawn unit transport for the final few miles. The speed of the advance depended on the ability of the railway engineers to push the railways forward so that the gap between the railheads and the leading troops was within the capacity of the road transport. When this gap reached the limit of the road transport's capability, the troops had to halt and await the advance of the railway or the improvement of the roads. Obviously if the roads were in good condition the distance over which vehicles could operate would be much greater than on bad roads.

On the day of the Armistice the railheads for the British Fourth Army were about fifty miles behind the leading troops, thus making the round trip by road about ninety miles for motor vehicles and, say, ten miles for animal transport. The other four British armies were better off, their railheads being between twenty and thirty miles from the cease-fire line. It had been found that during the advance the bad conditions of the roads due to enemy cratering, bridge-blowing and other demolitions, combined with the abnormally bad weather of the final week of operations, caused wear and tear to lorries far in excess of anything experienced previously.

Had the war continued the pace of the advance would have been governed largely by the state of the roads. As the winter weather and the mechanical condition of the lorries deteriorated, so the speed of the advance might be expected to become slower. The farther east the battle line advanced the more thorough enemy demolitions would have been. Had smaller forces been used to spearhead the advance the supply situation would, of course, have been eased. The British official

historian records that after the Armistice two of the five British
Armies, the Second and Fourth, comprising 32 divisions (about
half the total British strength), and the Cavalry Corps of 3
divisions, advanced to the German frontier, 11 divisions and
one cavalry division going on to the Rhine. All did so on full
rations. This gives some indication of what might have been
done, but the picture is an imperfect one and not a reliable
guide. The enemy had stopped fighting and had discontinued
his demolitions. With the cease-fire more civilian labour became
available to repair the roads. The quantities to be taken forward
were considerably reduced, being mostly confined to rations;
ammunition and other commodities wanted for fighting were
only required in very small quantities, if at all.

From this brief description of conditions we can conclude
that if the Allied Armies had been called upon to continue
fighting they had two courses open to them. They could have
advanced at full strength, in which case their advance would
have been slow and ponderous with frequent halts, of perhaps
several days, to bring the railway on and repair roads and
vehicles. Alternatively they could have gone forward at reduced
strength, but would have run the risk of being delayed, and
possibly halted, by the German rearguards.

The question is, could the German Army in either of these
circumstances have retained an unbroken front and prevented
the Allies from making any considerable incursions into
Germany? According to the diaries of Admiral Georg
Alexander von Müller (Chief of the Naval Cabinet, 1914–
1918) * the High Command when asked were non-commital,
but said they could not guarantee that the front would last for
three months. There is no doubt that the troops were exhausted
and morale declining; but it seems quite possible that, following
a further withdrawal to the frontier defences, the Germans
could have made a stand throughout the winter. But with the
resumption of fighting in the spring a decision in favour of the
Allies could not have been long delayed. By then the Allies
would have had vastly more American divisions and many

* The diaries form part of the book *The Kaiser and His Court*, edited by
Walter Görlitz and published in England in 1961.

more tanks: the Germans less men and probably a country in political chaos in rear of the battle front.

There can be no doubt that from the German point of view the decision to ask for an immediate Armistice was the correct one. It is conceivable that they could have gone on fighting for a little longer, but only at the expense of worse internal disorders and much worse Armistice and peace terms than they actually got.

CONCLUSION

As the Napoleonic wars saw the disappearance of comparatively small professional armies, and the beginning of large conscript infantry armies eventually deployed and supplied by railways, so the war of 1914–18 heralded the beginning of the era of highly mechanized fast-moving forces which reached its zenith in 1939–45. Today we still have the remnants of the old infantry armies, but spearheaded by highly mobile mechanized and airborne forces. Over all hangs the shadow of the nuclear missile, which for fear of the consequences both sides, in a regrouped world, maintain as a deterrent which they hope will never be used.

POSTSCRIPT

It has been said that 'the aim in war is to obtain a satisfactory peace', and, as a generalization, it is difficult to find a better definition.

When the fighting ended on 11th November 1918 there appeared to be every prospect of Britain and her Allies securing a good and lasting peace. The terms of the Armistice precluded any possibility of Germany resuming the struggle. It seemed that the victorious Allies could fashion a new world to their liking. Indeed the American President, Woodrow Wilson, had already shown the way in his 'Fourteen Points',* and his proposals for a League of Nations to control international relations and keep the world free from war.

Unfortunately these optimistic and idealistic hopes were not fulfilled. The inexperience of statesmen in solving the problems following a world war of the magnitude of that of 1914–18, and the weaknesses and follies of human nature, had been overlooked.

As a 'left-over' from the greater struggle, Britain found herself engaged in minor warlike activities in various parts of the world—in Afghanistan, in Russia in support of the White Russians against the Bolsheviks, and in acting as referees and peacemakers between Turks and Greeks. In Ireland a state of

* The 'Fourteen Points' are given in full in Appendix A.

open rebellion existed, and there was unrest in India. During most of the inter-war years Britain was to be plagued by industrial unrest, and in 1930 the country suffered a serious financial crisis.

The Peace Treaty—the Treaty of Versailles *—was signed on 28th June 1919. The subsequent refusal of the American Senate to ratify the Treaty, and America's consequent failure to join the League of Nations, deprived the League of the power and prestige necessary for its peace-keeping rôle throughout the inter-war years. It proved powerless to prevent Japanese aggression in China, Italian aggression in Abyssinia and Nazi Germany's many acts in violation of the Peace Treaty.

The international situation was further complicated by the rise and unpredictable future of Russia. In chaos at the time of the Armistice the Soviet Union recovered unexpectedly rapidly, and by the 1930s was on the path of development which was to bring her to the position in world affairs which she occupies today.

After the mid-1930s Hitler had openly repudiated the Treaty of Versailles and he and Mussolini were to openly defy the League. Neither it, nor the victorious Allies acting independently, had the will to stop aggression when it could have been stopped. By the time the democracies had mustered the resolution to call a halt it was too late. The two dictators made common cause, and so the Rome-Berlin Axis was born and the Second World War came about—less than twenty-one years after the Armistice of 1918 with its high hopes of peace and a better world.

* The Treaty of Versailles is explained and summarized in Appendix C.

THE 'FOURTEEN POINTS'

Extracts from President Wilson's Speech on
8th January 1918

The programme of the world's peace, therefore, is our programme, and that programme, the only possible programme,
as we see it, is this:

1. Open covenants of peace, openly arrived at, after which
there shall be no private international understandings of any
kind, but diplomacy shall proceed always frankly and in
public view.

2. Absolute freedom of navigation upon the seas, outside
territorial waters, alike in peace and in war, except as the seas
may be closed in whole or in part by international action for the
enforcements of international covenants.

3. The removal, so far as possible, of all economic barriers,
and the establishment of an equality of trade conditions among
all the nations consenting to the peace and associating themselves for its maintenance.

4. Adequate guarantees given and taken that national
armaments will be reduced to the lowest point consistent with
domestic safety.

5. A free, open-minded and absolutely impartial adjustment
of all colonial claims based upon a strict observance of the
principle that in determining all such questions of sovereignty
the interests of the populations concerned must have equal

weight with the equitable claims of the Government whose title is to be determined.

6. The evacuation of all Russian territory and such a settlement of all questions affecting Russia as will secure the best and freest co-operation of the other nations of the world in obtaining for her an unhampered and unembarrassed opportunity for the independent determination of her own political development and national policy, and assure her of a sincere welcome into the society of free nations under institutions of her own choosing, and, more than a welcome, assistance also of every kind that she may need and may herself desire. The treatment accorded Russia by her sister nations in the months to come will be the acid test of their goodwill, of their comprehension of her needs as distinguished from their own interests, and of their intelligent and unselfish sympathy.

7. Belgium, the whole world will agree, must be evacuated and restored without any attempt to limit the sovereignty which she enjoys in common with all other free nations. No other single act will serve to restore confidence among the nations in the laws which they have themselves set and determined for the government of their relations with one another. Without this healing act the whole structure and validity of international law is forever impaired.

8. All French territory should be freed, and the invaded portions restored, and the wrong done to France by Prussia in 1871, in the matter of Alsace-Lorraine, which has unsettled the peace of the world for nearly fifty years, should be righted in order that peace may once more be made secure in the interest of all.

9. A readjustment of the frontiers of Italy should be effected along clearly recognizable lines of nationality.

10. The peoples of Austro-Hungary, whose place among the nations we wish to see safeguarded and assured, should be accorded first opportunity of autonomous development.

11. Roumania, Serbia and Montenegro should be evacuated; occupied territories restored; Serbia accorded free and secure access to the sea; and the relations of the several Balkan states to one another determined by friendly counsel along historically

established lines of allegiance and nationality; and the international guarantees of the political and economic independence and territorial integrity of the several Balkan states should be entered into.

12. The Turkish portions of the present Ottoman Empire should be assured a secure sovereignty, but the other nationalities which are now under Turkish rule should be assured an undoubted security of life and an absolutely unmolested opportunity of autonomous development, and the Dardanelles should be permanently opened as a free passage to the ships and commerce of all nations under international guarantees.

13. An independent Polish state should be erected which should include the territories inhabited by indisputably Polish populations, which should be assured a free and secure access to the sea, and whose political and economic independence should be guaranteed by international covenant.

14. A general association of nations must be formed under specific covenants for the purpose of affording mutual guarantees of political independence and territorial integrity to great and small states alike.

APPENDIX B

THE ARMISTICE AGREEMENT WITH GERMANY

English Translation of the Agreement signed on 11th November 1918

BETWEEN Marshal Foch, Commander-in-Chief of the Allied Armies, acting on behalf of the Allied and Associated Powers, in conjunction with Admiral Wemyss, First Sea Lord, of the one part; and Secretary of State Erzberger, President of the German Delegation, Envoy Extraordinary and Minister Plenipotentiary Count von Oberndorff, Major-General von Winterfeldt, Captain Vanselow (German Navy), furnished with full powers in due form and acting with the approval of the German Chancellor, of the other part;

An Armistice has been concluded on the following conditions:

CONDITIONS OF THE ARMISTICE CONCLUDED WITH GERMANY

A. ON THE WESTERN FRONT

I. Cessation of hostilities on land and in the air six hours after the signature of the Armistice.

II. Immediate evacuation of the invaded countries: Belgium, France, Luxemburg, as well as Alsace-Lorraine, so ordered as to be completed within fifteen days from the signature of the Armistice. German troops which have not evacuated the above-mentioned territories within the period fixed will be made prisoners-of-war. Joint occupation by the Allied and United States forces shall keep pace with evacuation in these areas. All movements of evacuation or occupation shall be regulated in accordance with a Note (Annexe No. 1), drawn up at the time of signature of the Armistice.

III. Repatriation, beginning at once, to be completed within fifteen days of all inhabitants of the countries above enumerated (including hostages, persons under trial or convicted).

IV. Surrender in good condition by the German armies of the following war material:

 5,000 guns (2,500 heavy, 2,500 field)
 25,000 machine-guns
 3,000 trench mortars
 1,700 fighting and bombing aeroplanes—in the first place, all D 7's and all night-bombing aeroplanes.

The above to be delivered *in situ* to the Allied and United States troops in accordance with the detailed conditions laid down in the Note (Annexe No. 1) determined at the time of the signing of the Armistice.

V. Evacuation by the German armies of the districts on the left bank of the Rhine. These districts on the left bank of the Rhine shall be administered by the local authorities under the control of the Allied and United States Armies of Occupation.

The occupation of these territories by Allied and United States troops shall be assured by garrisons holding the principal crossings of the Rhine (Mainz, Coblenz, Cologne), together with bridge-heads at these points of a 30-kilometre (about 19 miles) radius on the right bank, and by garrisons similarly holding the strategic points of the area.

A neutral zone shall be reserved on the right bank of the Rhine, between the river and a line drawn parallel to the bridge-heads and to the river and 10 kilometres (6¼ miles) distant from them, between the Dutch frontier and the Swiss frontier.

The evacuation by the enemy of the Rhine districts (right and left banks) shall be so ordered as to be completed within a further period of 16 days, in all 31 days after the signing of the Armistice.

All movements of evacuation and occupation shall be regulated according to the Note (Annexe No. 1) determined at the time of the signing of the Armistice.

VI. In all territories evacuated by the enemy, evacuation of the inhabitants shall be forbidden; no damage or harm shall be done to the persons or property of the inhabitants.

No person shall be prosecuted for having taken part in any military measures previous to the signing of the Armistice.

No destruction of any kind to be committed.

Military establishments of all kinds shall be delivered intact, as well as military stores, food, munitions and equipment, which shall not have been removed during the periods fixed for evacuation.

Stores of food of all kinds for the civil population, cattle, etc., shall be left *in situ*.

No measure of a general character shall be taken, and no official order shall be given which would have as a consequence the depreciation of industrial establishments or a reduction of their personnel.

VII. Roads and means of communications of every kind, railroads, waterways, roads, bridges, telegraphs, telephones, shall be in no manner impaired.

All civil and military personnel at present employed on them shall remain.

5,000 locomotives and 150,000 wagons, in good working order, with all necessary spare parts and fittings, shall be delivered to the associated powers within the period fixed in Annexe No. 2 (not exceeding 31 days in all).

5,000 motor lorries are also to be delivered in good condition within 36 days.

The railways of Alsace-Lorraine shall be handed over within 31 days, together with all personnel and material belonging to the organization of this system.

Further, the necessary working material in the territories on the left bank of the Rhine shall be left *in situ*.

IWUY. Marshal Foch and Field-Marshal Sir Douglas Haig inspecting a Guard of Honour of the 6th Battalion the Gordon Highlanders, 15th November 1918.

COMPIÈGNE. Marshal Foch's train arriving at the station on 11th November 1918. It was in this train that the Armistice was signed. Hitler, in dramatic style, caused this train to be produced at the same place for the signing of the Armistice with France in 1940.

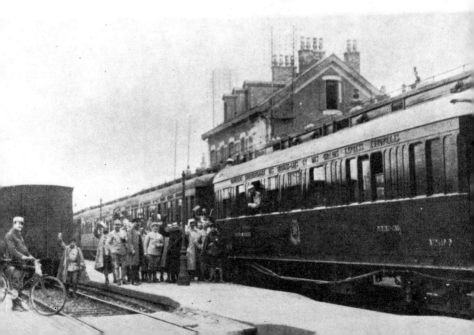

METZ. Presentation to Marshal Pétain (in front) of the Baton of a
Marshal of France, 8th December 1918. Behind Pétain (left to right):
Marshals Joffre and Foch; Field-Marshal Sir Douglas Haig; Generals
Pershing (U.S.A.), Gillain (Belgium), Albricci (Italy) and Haller
(Poland).

DOVER. The
mayor and
corporation
receiving
President Wilson
on 26th Decem-
ber 1918.

All stores of coal and material for the upkeep of permanent way, signals and repair shops shall be left *in situ* and kept in an efficient state by Germany, so far as the working of the means of communications on the left bank of the Rhine is concerned.

All lighters taken from the Allies shall be restored to them.

The Note (Annexe No. 1) defines the details of these measures.

VIII. The German Command shall be responsible for revealing within 48 hours after the signing of the Armistice, all mines or delay-action fuses disposed on territories evacuated by the German troops and shall assist in their discovery and destruction.

The German Command shall also reveal all destructive measures that may have been taken (such as poisoning or pollution of wells, springs, etc.).

Breaches of these clauses will involve reprisals.

IX. The right of requisition shall be exercised by the Allied and United States armies in all occupied territories, save for settlement of accounts with authorized persons.

The upkeep of the troops of occupation in the Rhine districts (excluding Alsace-Lorraine) shall be charged to the German Government.

X. The immediate repatriation, without reciprocity, according to detailed conditions which shall be fixed, of all Allied and United States prisoners-of-war, including those under trial and condemned. The Allied powers and the United States of America shall be able to dispose of these prisoners as they think fit. This condition annuls all other conventions regarding prisoners-of-war, including that of July 1918, now being ratified. However, the return of German prisoners-of-war interned in Holland and Switzerland shall continue as heretofore. The return of German prisoners-of-war shall be settled at the conclusion of the peace preliminaries.

XI. Sick and wounded who cannot be removed from territory evacuated by the German forces shall be cared for by German personnel, who shall be left on the spot with the material required.

B. CLAUSES RELATING TO THE EASTERN FRONTIERS OF GERMANY

xii. All German troops at present in any territory which before the war formed part of Austria-Hungary, Roumania or Turkey, shall withdraw within the frontiers of Germany as they existed on 1st August 1914, and all German troops at present in territories which before the war formed part of Russia, must likewise return to within the frontiers of Germany as above defined, as soon as the Allies shall think the moment suitable, having regard to the internal situation of these territories.

xiii. Evacuation of German troops to begin at once, and all German instructors, prisoners and agents, civilian as well as military, now on the territory of Russia (frontiers as defined on 1st August 1914) to be recalled.

xiv. German troops to cease at once all requisitions and seizures and any other coercive measures with a view to obtaining supplies intended for Germany in Roumania and Russia (frontiers as defined on 1st August 1914).

xv. Annulment of the treaties of Bucharest and Brest-Litovsk and of the supplementary treaties.

xvi. The Allies shall have free access to the territories evacuated by the Germans on their Eastern frontier, either through Danzig or by the Vistula, in order to convey supplies to the populations of these territories or for the purpose of maintaining order.

C. CLAUSE RELATING TO EAST AFRICA

xvii. Evacuation of all German forces operating in East Africa within a period specified by the Allies.

D. GENERAL CLAUSES

xviii. Repatriation without reciprocity, within a maximum period of one month, in accordance with detailed conditions hereafter to be fixed, of all interned civilians, including hostages and persons under trial and condemned, who may be subjects of Allied or associated states other than those mentioned in Clause III.

XIX. *Financial Clauses*

With the reservation that any subsequent concessions and claims by the Allies and United States remain unaffected, the following financial conditions are imposed:

Reparation for damage done.

While the Armistice lasts, no public securities shall be removed by the enemy which can serve as a pledge to the Allies to cover reparation for war losses.

Immediate restitution of the cash deposit in the National Bank of Belgium and, in general, immediate return of all documents, specie, stocks, shares, paper money, together with plant for the issue thereof, affecting public or private interests in the invaded countries.

Restitution of the Russian and Roumanian gold yielded to Germany or taken by that power.

This gold to be delivered in trust to the Allies until peace is concluded.

E. NAVAL CONDITIONS

XX. Immediate cessation of all hostilities at sea, and definite information to be given as to the position and movements of all German ships.

Notification to be given to neutrals that freedom of navigation in all territorial waters is given to the Navies and Mercantile Marines of the Allied and associated powers, all questions of neutrality being waived.

XXI. All naval and mercantile marine prisoners-of-war of the Allied and associated powers in German hands to be returned without reciprocity.

XXII. To surrender at the ports specified by the Allies and the United States all submarines at present in existence (including all submarine cruisers and mine-layers), with armament and equipment complete. Those that cannot put to sea shall be deprived of armament and equipment, and shall remain under the supervision of the Allies and the United States. Submarines ready to put to sea shall be prepared to leave German ports immediately on receipt of a wireless order to sail to the port of surrender, the remainder to follow as early as possible. The conditions of this Article shall be completed within 14 days of the signing of the Armistice.

xxiii. The following German surface warships, which shall be designated by the Allies and the United States of America, shall forthwith be disarmed and thereafter interned in neutral ports, or, failing them, Allied ports, to be designated by the Allies and the United States of America, and placed under the surveillance of the Allies and the United States of America, only care and maintenance parties being left on board, namely:

   6 battle cruisers,
  10 battleships,
   8 light cruisers (including two minelayers),
  50 destroyers of the most modern type.

All other surface warships (including river craft) are to be concentrated in German Naval bases, to be designated by the Allies and the United States of America, completely disarmed and placed under the supervision of the Allies and the United States of America. All vessels of the Auxiliary Fleet are to be disarmed. All vessels specified for internment shall be ready to leave German ports seven days after the signing of the Armistice. Directions for the voyage shall be given by wireless.

xxiv. The Allies and the United States of America shall have the right to sweep up all minefields and destroy all obstructions laid by Germany outside German territorial waters, and the positions of these are to be indicated.

xxv. Freedom of access to and from the Baltic to be given to the Navies and Mercantile Marines of the Allied and Associated Powers. This to be secured by the occupation of all German forts, fortifications, batteries and defence works of all kinds in all the routes from the Cattegat into the Baltic, and by the sweeping up and destruction of all mines and obstructions within and without German territorial waters without any questions of neutrality being raised by Germany, and the positions of all such mines and obstructions to be indicated, and the plans relating thereto are to be supplied.

XXVI. The existing blockade conditions set up by the Allied and Associated Powers are to remain unchanged, and all German merchant ships found at sea are to remain liable to capture. The Allies and United States contemplate the provisioning of Germany during the Armistice as shall be found necessary.

XXVII. All aerial forces are to be concentrated and immobilized in German bases to be specified by the Allies and the United States of America.

XXVIII. In evacuating the Belgian coasts and ports, Germany shall abandon, *in situ* and intact, the port material and material for inland waterways, also all merchant ships, tugs and lighters, all Naval aircraft and air materials and stores, all arms and armaments and all stores and apparatus of all kinds.

XXIX. All Black Sea ports are to be evacuated by Germany; all Russian warships of all descriptions seized by Germany in the Black Sea are to be handed over to the Allies and the United States of America; all neutral merchant ships seized in the Black Sea are to be released; all warlike and other materials of all kinds seized in those parts are to be returned, and German materials as specified in Clause XXVIII are to be abandoned.

XXX. All merchant ships at present in German hands belonging to the Allied and Associated Powers are to be restored to ports specified by the Allies and the United States of America without reciprocity.

XXXI. No destruction of ships or of materials to be permitted before evacuation, surrender or restoration.

XXXII. The German Government shall formally notify all the neutral Governments, and particularly the Governments of Norway, Sweden, Denmark and Holland, that all restrictions placed on the trading of their vessels with the Allied and Associated countries, whether by the German Government or by private German interests, and whether in return for specific concessions, such as the export of shipbuilding materials, or not, are immediately cancelled.

XXXIII. No transfers of German merchant shipping of any description to any neutral flag are to take place after signature of the Armistice.

F. DURATION OF ARMISTICE

XXXIV. The duration of the Armistice is to be 36 days, with option to extend. During this period, on failure of execution of any of the above clauses, the Armistice may be repudiated by one of the contracting parties on 48 hours' previous notice. It is understood that failure to execute Articles III and XVIII completely in the periods specified is not to give reason for a repudiation of the Armistice, save where such failure is due to malice aforethought.

To ensure the execution of the present convention under the most favourable conditions, the principle of a permanent International Armistice Commission is recognized. This Commission shall act under the supreme authority of the High Command, military and naval, of the Allied Armies.

The present Armistice was signed on the 11th day of November 1918, at 5 o'clock a.m. (French time)

(Signed)

F. Foch	*Erzberger*
R. E. Wemyss	*Oberndorff*
	Winterfeldt
	Vanselow

11th November 1918

The representatives of the Allies declare that in view of fresh events, it appears necessary to them that the following condition shall be added to the clauses of the Armistice:

In case the German ships are not handed over within the periods specified, the governments of the Allies and of the

United States shall have the right to occupy Heligoland to ensure their delivery.

(Signed)

R. E. Wemyss.   *F. Foch*

Admiral

The German delegates declare that they will forward this declaration to the German Chancellor, with the recommendation that it be accepted, accompanying it with the reasons by which the Allies have been actuated in making this demand.

(Signed)

Erzberger

Oberndorff

Winterfeldt

Vanselow

ANNEXE NO. I

1. The evacuation of the invaded territories, Belgium, France and Luxemburg, and also of Alsace-Lorraine, shall be carried out in three successive stages according to the following conditions:

1st stage.—Evacuation of the territories situated between the existing front and line No. 1 on the enclosed map,* to be completed within 5 days after the signature of the Armistice.

2nd stage.—Evacuation of territories situated between line No. 1 and line No. 2 to be carried out within 4 further days (9 days in all after the signing of the Armistice).

3rd stage.—Evacuation of the territories situated between line No. 2 and line No. 3, to be completed within 6 further days (15 days in all after the signing of the Armistice).

Allied and United States troops shall enter these various territories on the expiration of the period allowed to the German troops for the evacuation of each.

* Map not included in the Appendix.

In consequence, the Allied troops will cross the present German front as from the 6th day following the signing of the Armistice, line No. 1 as from the 10th day, and line No. 2 as from the 16th day.

II. *Evacuation of the Rhine district.*—This evacuation shall also be carried out in several successive stages:

1. Evacuation of territories situated between lines 2 and 3 and line 4 to be completed within 4 further days (19 days in all after the signing of the Armistice).

2. Evacuation of territories situated between lines 4 and 5 to be completed within 4 further days (23 days in all after the signing of the Armistice).

3. Evacuation of territories situated between lines 5 and 6 (line of the Rhine) to be completed within 4 further days (27 days in all after the signing of the Armistice).

4. Evacuation of the bridge-heads and of the neutral zone on the right bank of the Rhine to be completed within 4 further days (31 days in all after the signing of the Armistice).

The Allied and United States Army of Occupation shall enter these various territories after the expiration of the period allowed to the German troops for the evacuation of each; consequently the army will cross line No. 3, 20 days after the signing of the Armistice. It will cross line No. 4 as from the 24th day after the signing of the Armistice; line No. 5 as from the 28th day; line No. 6 (Rhine) the 32nd day, in order to occupy the bridge-heads.

III. *Surrender by the German armies of war material specified by the Armistice.*—This war material shall be surrendered according to the following conditions: The first half before the 10th day, the second half before the 20th day. This material shall be handed over to each of the Allied and United States Armies by each larger tactical group of the German Armies in the proportions which may be fixed by the permanent International Armistice Commission.

ANNEXE NO. 2

Conditions regarding communications, railways, waterways, roads, river and sea ports and telegraphic and telephonic communications:

I. All communications as far as the Rhine, inclusive or comprised, on the right bank of this river, within the bridge-heads occupied by the Allied Armies shall be placed under the supreme and absolute authority of the Commander-in-Chief of the Allied Armies, who shall have the right to take any measure he may think necessary to assure their occupation and use. All documents relative to communications shall be held ready for transmission to him.

II. All the material and all the civil and military personnel at present employed in the maintenance and working of all lines of communication are to be maintained in their entirety upon these lines in all territories evacuated by the German troops.

All supplementary material necessary for the upkeep of these lines of communication in the districts on the left bank of the Rhine shall be supplied by the German Government throughout the duration of the Armistice.

III. *Personnel.*—The French and Belgian personnel belonging to the services of the lines of communication, whether interned or not, are to be returned to the French and Belgian armies during the 15 days following the signing of the Armistice. The personnel belonging to the organization of the Alsace-Lorraine railway system is to be maintained or reinstated in such a way as to ensure the working of the system.

The Commander-in-Chief of the Allied Armies shall have the right to make all changes and substitutions that he may desire in the personnel of the lines of communication.

IV. *Material*

(a) *Rolling stock.*—The rolling stock handed over to the Allied Armies in the zone comprised between the present front and line No. 3, not including Alsace-Lorraine, shall amount at least to 5,000 locomotives and 150,000 wagons. This surrender shall be carried out within the period fixed by Clause VII of the Armistice and under conditions, the details of which shall be fixed by the permanent International Armistice Commission.

All this material is to be in good condition and in working order with all the ordinary spare parts and fittings. It may be employed together with the regular personnel, or with any other, upon any part of the railway system of the Allied Armies.

The material necessary for the working of the Alsace-Lorraine railway system is to be maintained or replaced for the use of the French Army.

The material to be left *in situ* in the territories on the left bank of the Rhine, as well as that on the inner side of the bridge-heads, must permit of the normal working of the railways in these districts.

(*b*) *Permanent way, signals and workshops.*—The material for signals, machine tools and tool outfits, taken from the workshops and depôts of the French and Belgian lines, are to be replaced under conditions, the details of which are to be arranged by the permanent International Armistice Commission.

The Allied Armies are to be supplied with railroad material, rails, incidental fittings, plant, bridge-building material and timber necessary for the repair of the lines destroyed beyond the present front.

(*c*) *Fuel and maintenance material.*—The German Government shall be responsible throughout the duration of the Armistice for the release of fuel and maintenance material to the depôts normally allotted to the railways in the territories on the left bank of the Rhine.

v. *Telegraphic and Telephonic Communications.*—All telegraphs, telephones and fixed W/T stations are to be handed over to the Allied Armies, with all the civil and military personnel and all their material, including all stores on the left bank of the Rhine.

Supplementary stores necessary for the upkeep of the system are to be supplied throughout the duration of the Armistice by the German Government according to requirements.

The Commander-in-Chief of the Allied Armies shall place

this system under military supervision and shall ensure its control, and shall make all changes and substitutions in personnel which he may think necessary.

He will send back to the German Army all the military personnel who are not in his judgement necessary for the working and upkeep of the railway.

All plans of the German telegraphic and telephonic systems shall be handed over to the Commander-in-Chief of the Allied Armies.

Note. Later three Conventions were signed prolonging the Armistice and making certain amendments of detail:

I. *On 13th December 1918*, prolonging it until 5 a.m. on 17th January 1919.

II. *On 16th January 1919*, prolonging it until 5 a.m. on 17th February 1919, and making a number of minor amendments.

III. *On 16th February 1919*, prolonging it for an unspecified period, and making an additional agreement requiring the Germans to cease hostilities against the Poles at once.

APPENDIX C

THE PEACE TREATY BETWEEN THE ASSOCIATED POWERS AND GERMANY

The Treaty of Versailles, 1919

(SEE MAPS VI(A), VI(B))

NOTES AND SUMMARY

Notes

(a) In January 1919 the plenipotentiaries of the Allied and associated powers met at Versailles to draw up peace conditions with the defeated central powers. (This Appendix is concerned only with that part of the Treaty dealing with peace with Germany.)

(b) Although representatives from many countries attended, the main work of the Conference was carried out by a Council of Ten, consisting of two representatives each from Britain, France, United States, Italy and Japan. Later most of the work was done by a Council of Four and later still by the 'Big Three'—Wilson, Clemenceau and Lloyd George, after Orlando (Italy) had withdrawn. The British Empire delegation consisted of Lloyd George, Balfour, Bonar Law, G. N. Barnes and from time to time members of the panel of Dominion Premiers. The Dominions had delegations of their own at the Conference.

(c) The draft of the Treaty was presented to the German delegates on 7th May 1919. On 22nd June the German National Assembly at Weimar voted in favour of acceptance—by a majority of 99 (237 for and 138 against), and on 28th June the German representatives signed the Treaty at Versailles.

(d) In the forefront of the Treaty were the proposed conditions for establishing a League of Nations, under which the contracting parties were to achieve international peace and security by:

(1) The acceptance of obligations not to resort to war.

(2) The prescription of open, just and honourable relations between nations.

(3) The firm establishment of the understandings of international law as the actual rule and conduct among governments.

(4) The maintenance of justice and a scrupulous respect for all treaty obligations in the dealings of organized peoples with one another.

The above principles were explained in detail in the 26 Articles which comprised the text of the proposed Covenant of the League.

An Annexure to the League Covenant gave a list of participating nations, as follows:

Original Members of the League of Nations Signatories of the Treaty of Peace:

United States of America	China
Belgium	Cuba
Bolivia	Ecuador
Brazil	France
British Empire:	Greece
Canada	Guatemala
Australia	Haiti
South Africa	Hedjaz
New Zealand	Honduras
India	Portugal
Italy	Rumania

Japan	Serb-Croat-Slovene State
Liberia	(now known as Yugoslavia)
Nicaragua	Siam
Panama	Czechoslovakia
Peru	Uruguay
Poland	

States Invited to Accede to the Covenant:

Argentine	Persia
Chile	Salvador
Colombia	Spain
Denmark	Sweden
Netherlands	Switzerland
Norway	Venezuela
Paraguay	

The first Secretary General of the League of Nations was the Honourable Sir James Eric Drummond.

Although she appears at the top of the list, and her President Wilson originated the idea of the League of Nations, the American Senate failed to ratify the Treaty of Versailles—mainly because of the objection of a majority of members to the Covenant of the League.

The Covenant of the League is followed by the main body of the Treaty—beginning with the Treaty with Germany of which the following is a summary:

SUMMARY OF THE PEACE TREATY BETWEEN THE ASSOCIATED POWERS AND GERMANY

Main territories surrendered by Germany *

Alsace-Lorraine to France.

Most of the Provinces of West Prussia and Posen to Poland.

A substantial part of East Silesia and East Prussia to Poland.

A part of Upper Silesia to Czechoslovakia.

---

* These are the most important territories surrendered. For the post-Treaty map of Europe see Map No. vi(b).

Memel to Lithuania.

Danzig to be a free city and port under the League of Nations.

Part of Schleswig to Denmark.

All Germany's overseas possessions to be renounced in favour of the principal Allied and associated powers.

Main military and naval clauses

Germany was forbidden to construct fortifications on either bank of a large section of the Rhine.

Allied troops to occupy all German territory west of the Rhine, together with certain bridge-heads on the east bank, for fifteen years. (Or less in certain cases and conditions.)

The German Army to be limited to 100,000 officers and men, organized in 7 infantry and 3 cavalry divisions; no tanks permitted. Men to serve for a minimum of twelve years, thus making it difficult to build up a large and efficient reserve.

The German Navy to be limited to 15,000 officers and men. No Air Force permitted.

The General Staff, as it had existed before and during the war, to be abolished, and Germany forbidden to maintain a Staff College or similar establishment for the study of the higher direction of war or higher staff procedure.

REPARATIONS

Germany and her allies to accept responsibility for causing all the loss and damage to which the Allied and Associated Powers had been subjected as a consequence of the war.

Germany to pay 20,000,000,000 gold marks, in instalments, pending a final assessment by a Reparations Commission. In addition certain commodities and livestock to be handed over in kind to the Allied and Associated Powers. Buildings and household goods destroyed or damaged in the occupied territories to be rebuilt or replaced. Germany to replace ton for ton, and class for class, all merchant and fishing ships lost or damaged during the war.

MAP VI(A). Europe before World War I, 1914

Germany to pay for the Allied Armies of occupation in Germany.

Germany to give every assistance and co-operation to the Reparations Commission in carrying out its duties.

PENALTIES

The Allied and associated powers publicly arraigned William II of Hohenzollern, formerly German Emperor, for a supreme offence against international morality and the sanctity of treaties. A special Tribunal to be constituted to try the accused,

MAP VI(B). Europe after World War I, 1920,
as a result of the Versailles Treaty

to be composed of five judges, one from each of the following
countries—U.S.A., Great Britain, France, Italy and Japan.
The Allied and Associated Powers to address a request to the
Government of the Netherlands for the surrender of the
ex-Emperor.

The German Government to recognize the right of the
Allied and Associated Powers to bring before military tribunals
persons accused of acts in violation of the laws and customs of war.
Such persons to be handed over on request by the German
Government to the Allied and Associated Powers, or any one of
them.

MISCELLANEOUS

Germany to accept the abrogation of the Treaties of Brest-Litovsk and all other treaties, conventions and agreements entered into by her with the Maximalist Government in Russia.

There were also provisions relating to labour organizations, trade and economic conditions, aerial navigation, ports and waterways, the disposal of German property in Allied countries, etc.

Notes

(a) The portion of the Treaty concerning Germany was followed by treaties between the Allied and Associated Powers and Austria and Bulgaria. (A separate Peace Treaty was negotiated with Turkey—the Treaty of Sèvres, signed on 10th August 1920.)

(b) The whole Treaty of Versailles contains some 440 Articles. It was presented to the British Parliament as Treaty Series No. 4 (1919) Cmnd 153.

(c) Many of the Articles of the Treaty were not implemented —indeed it was notable more in the breach than in the observance. The Kaiser was never tried, as the Government of the Netherlands declined to surrender him to the Allies; reparations were never paid in full and many of the most important articles were abrogated by Hitler by unilateral action. The earliest, and perhaps the greatest, blow was the non-ratification by the United States. Without America as a member, the League of Nations started its existence at half-cock and was unable to exercise the influence on world affairs for which it was originally designed.

INDEX